Bruce

Loved and Lost
Govanhill's Built Heritage

About the Author

Bruce Downie is a local historian, tour guide and author of *Loved and Lost: Govanhill's Built Heritage* published in 2019 and *99 Calder Street: A History of Govanhill Baths and Washhouse* published in 2021.

Govanhill Baths Community Trust, through its Archive and Heritage Programme, commissioned Bruce to write these books.

Acknowledgements

The author would like to thank:

Glasgow City Archives and Special Collections and all the staff at the Mitchell Library, NHS Greater Glasgow and Clyde Archive, Glasgow University Archive, Scottish Jewish Archives Centre, Glasgow Police Museum, SFA Football Museum, Glasgow School of Art Library, Arlington Baths Club History Group, Govanhill Housing Association, Harvey Kaplan, Fiona Brodie, Dave Zagieba, Ken MacDougall, Sheila Halley at The Dixon Community, John Oates, Gary Painter, Bruce Gilmour, Paula Larkin who secured copyright for all the images, Fatima Uygun who managed the project, Julian Dawydiak who designed this book, and Rebecca Livesey-Wright who coordinated the first edition of this book.

Special thanks to the community members who attended the Govanhill Heritage Meet-Up Group to share their memories, anecdotes, thoughts and advice; Saskia McCracken, John Cooper, Lindsey Duncan, Peter Fletcher, Alex Shannon and Vincent McGowan.

We would like to extend sincere thanks to Historic Environment Scotland for funding the production of the first edition.

For the second edition, special thanks are due to Pat McGeady for his contribution to the Third Lanark chapter. Also, the British Newspaper Archive has also been an invaluable research tool, providing additional information that has enhanced several chapters.

First published 2019

This revised edition published 2022

ISBN: 978-1-3999-2892-2

Govanhill Baths Community Trust
99 Calder Street
Govanhill
Glasgow
G42 7RA
www.govanhillbaths.com

Govanhill Baths Community Trust is registered as a Scottish Charity No. SC036162.
Registered Office: 99 Calder Street, Govanhill, Glasgow, G42 7RA.

Design and layout by Julian Dawydiak

Loved and Lost

Govanhill's Built Heritage

—— Revised and Expanded ——

Bruce Downie

Govanhill Baths Community Trust Publication

Contents

Preface

The origin of this project can be traced back to the campaign to save one of the most iconic buildings on the south side of Glasgow, Govanhill Baths on Calder Street. In 2001, the local community, led by the 'Save Our Pool' campaign, fought heroically to save the baths. The historic occupation of the building lasted 147 days and marked the beginning of a long struggle to preserve a vital and much-loved community asset. The refurbishment and restoration of Govanhill Baths to its former glory will be completed in 2023.

Since the establishment of Govanhill Baths Community Trust in 2004, we have worked hard to inspire and empower our community by providing a wide range of services, classes, events and opportunities. One part of that mission has been to establish and build a community archive, to celebrate and raise awareness of the rich history and heritage of Govanhill. This book serves the same purpose.

Foreword

Loved and Lost began with the idea to explore the built heritage of Govanhill, to rediscover the history of some of the buildings, businesses and places that have formed an important part of our shared story. Some of the places featured in this book have long since been demolished in the name of progress, other places still stand but have been repurposed and renewed. If we are lucky, we can find a few records, a few stories of what went on within those walls in the past and so cherish and preserve a vital and vibrant part of our local history.

Brush away the cobwebs of history and it is possible to find some fascinating stories that have happened in and around Govanhill, events and developments that have given this area a unique and distinct identity.

Govanhill is so much more than just a suburb of Glasgow. For many years it was a fiercely independent community, with few laws and little regulation. Subsequently, it became an independent burgh with the right to manage its own affairs, free from outside control, before finally, reluctantly, agreeing to become part of Glasgow.

Glasgow may have enjoyed the status of 'second city' of the Empire but so much that has happened within or close to Govanhill has helped shape Glasgow and contribute to its reputation. There are great examples of industry, engineering, heath care, municipal projects, culture and entertainment that have made Govanhill great, including shipbuilding, despite being half a mile from the River Clyde. In addition, Govanhill still contains some of the best examples of working-class tenement housing standing in Glasgow today, some built by the renowned Scottish architect Alexander 'Greek' Thompson.

This book goes a little beyond the boundaries of present-day Govanhill. It is impossible to ignore the impact and influence of the surrounding districts, especially Crosshill, but also Pollokshields, Strathbungo and the Gorbals.

The boundaries of all those districts have ebbed and flowed over the years. City, county, parish, burgh and parliamentary boundaries have moved one way, then another, to suit the times. People's lives do not fit neatly into borders prescribed by a politician, a line drawn down the middle of a street. People can live and work in different districts and visit family in yet another. So, while this book starts with Govanhill, it embraces a slightly larger area, one that defies restriction or definition. This fantastic place to live and work, love and laugh, is a part of Glasgow that has given so much to the city and that has meant the world to so many people.

Introduction

In the 12th century, King David I of Scotland gifted the lands on the south side of the River Clyde, the lands between Renfrew and Rutherglen, to the newly established archdiocese in Glasgow. In addition, he also gifted lands on the north side of the river, lying to the west of Glasgow, principally the lands of old Partick.

Under the authority of the reestablished Archbishopric of Glasgow, these lands became known as the Parish of Govan. There were already at least two well-established villages within the parish, Meikle Govan, two miles west of Glasgow, which we know today as the district of Govan, and another village called Little Govan, which was much closer to Glasgow, on the south side of the river.

Little Govan has long gone, no trace remains, but it was situated in present day Oatlands, just east of what is now the Southern Necropolis, and it was the principle village within an estate called the Lands of Little Govan, which was bordered on the north by the River Clyde, on the west by the Lands of Gorbals, on the east by the Lands of Polmadie and on the south by the Lands of Crosshill.

The Blind Burn separated the Lands of Little Govan from Gorbals; the Polmadie Burn, or what would later be known as Jenny's Burn, formed the boundary with Polmadie and the Crosshill Burn formed the southern boundary.

Just south of the village of Little Govan, was a hill that was the highest hill within the entire parish, and that hill became known as Govan Hill. Today, the top of that hill can be found where Govanhill Street meets Hollybrook Street.

In the early 18th century, just to the south of Govan Hill, coal was discovered, and a colliery was established that became known as the Little Govan Colliery. At the time, it was owned and operated by the Rae family, who owned most of the Lands of Little Govan.

In 1764, Colin Rae, the principle at the time, sold all his pits and mine shafts for £8,000, to Colin Dunlop and Alexander Houston, who also owned land locally. Then, in the 1790s, Dunlop and Houston hired a young Englishman called William Dixon to manage the colliery, Dixon eventually became a partner, and then the sole owner of the colliery and much of the surrounding land.

At first, Dixon lived in the manager's house within the colliery yard, known as Bankhall House, which gave its name to present day Bankhall Street, but around 1795, he built a house on top of Govan Hill that became known as Govanhill House, and the land around the hill which was known as the Govanhill Estate.

Over time, the colliery became more successful, and Dixon needed more people to work for him, so he built cottages in and around the colliery yard. Most of these cottages became known as the 'Houses of Fireworks' or 'Fireworks Village' because of the sparks made by the steam engine that Dixon used in the colliery, to bring coal up from the surface.

There were other cottages around the colliery that were not occupied by miners but by labourers and agricultural workers who had other jobs in the area. In the 1841 census, the first full census in Scotland, there were three cottages, home to just three families and 13 people, that were listed as part of the village of Govan Hill. Just a stone's throw south of the village of Govan Hill, was Fireworks Village, which was home to 694 people, mostly miners and their families, and just south of Fireworks, just over the county boundary, was a small village called Crosshill, built around a freestone quarry, which was home to just 64 people.

Over the next 30 years or so, Dixon's enterprise grew more extensive, there were several mineshafts locally, there were still farms and nurseries, but more and more people were coming to live in the area, more dwellings were required, and no single name became the established name for the neighbourhood.

As far as the Ordnance Survey in 1858 was concerned, the area was simply and functionally called Colliery Works. The census report of 1861 reverted to the old name of Little Govan, even though the village of Little Govan had been demolished several decades earlier, and a section of Cathcart Road even became a recognisable place or village, in its own right, for a few short years.

Because of increasing concerns about health and sanitation in the 19th century, legislation was passed in Parliament in the 1830s, and was further refined in the 1850s and 1860s, which aimed to bring every settlement with a sizable population under municipal control, to make them part of larger municipalities or independent police burghs.

In 1862, when the Police Burgh (Scotland) Act was passed, the area in and around the Little Govan Colliery, did not yet have a sufficient population to qualify for burgh status, so it was referred to, at least officially, as No Man's Land.

This was not a unique title, there were pockets of land around Glasgow, and around the country, which became known by the same name for a while (one hamlet in Devon still is known as Nomansland) but as the population around the colliery and the iron works grew, the name No Man's Land became well-established, and was perhaps, for some, even a source of pride.

Crosshill, to the south, had become a self-governing burgh in 1871, and spent time and money trying to absorb No Man's Land, to make it part of Crosshill. Glasgow, just to the north, also wanted to claim the disputed area of No Man's Land for itself. Crosshill almost succeeded in 1875, the Crosshill Annexation Bill, got to a third reading in Parliament, but it was finally dismissed because of the strength of the opposition from Glasgow.

The inhabitants of No Man's Land wanted to remain independent, they did not want to pay extra rates to Glasgow or Crosshill, but they knew that they needed to be better organised, able to deal with local issues like sanitation and lighting, and to have their own fire brigade and police force. In 1877, the population had reached 8,000, more than enough to become a burgh, but by then, the increasingly prosperous and respectable residents were not going to call themselves No Man's Land, they needed to find a slightly more respectable name.

On the 4th of July 1877, a meeting, chaired by the Sheriff of Lanark, was held in new Candlish Church, on the corner of Calder Street and Cathcart Road, where local residents voted to become a burgh under the terms the 1862 Police Burgh Act and to choose a new name.

Deferential appellations like Dixontown and Dixon Land were considered, to honour the Dixon family, but William Smith Dixon, the grandson of the man who had brought so much industry to the area, declined that mark of respect. Other options put forward included Broadlands, Queen's Burgh, Victoria, and Beaconsfield, but the name chosen finally by an overwhelming majority of residents, was a name that had been strongly associated with the area for at least 80 – Govanhill.

The Burgh of Govanhill

In the early 1870s, Glasgow and the newly-formed Burgh of Crosshill, wanted to absorb the disputed area that lay between them, known as No Man's Land, into their boundaries, but the inhabitants of that area had different ideas. Most of the population lived on, or near Cathcart Road, and many worked in the nearby collieries, in the iron foundry known as Dixon's Blazes or in the engineering or locomotive building industry in Polmadie.

The population of No Man's Land continued to grow in the 1870s and became more diverse but the residents continued to be proud of their independence, their commercial freedom, their industrial significance and were determined to remain distinct from Glasgow and Crosshill.

There was very likely a tense, difficult relationship throughout the early part of the decade between Crosshill and No Man's Land. They were physically different spaces, with different population profiles and different priorities, and even when the area became the Burgh of Govanhill in 1877, it was unlikely that all those differences would have been resolved or forgotten. Yet common cause and shared interests were discovered, and at the opening of the Crosshill and Govanhill Burgh Hall in 1879, Provost Hunter of Govanhill, spoke of finally *'living in harmony with all around.'*

The two new burghs had power to borrow money from the government and to raise money through rates. Some of their early priorities included street lighting, gas, sanitation, cleansing and employing a police force and fire brigade. Govanhill built a police station in what is now known as Belleisle House, behind Dixon Halls, but Crosshill being in a different county, continued to rely on the Renfrewshire Police Force. Govanhill had their own hand-drawn fire cart and later a horse-drawn fire cart. Crosshill's fire brigade did not have a cart, but being a relatively small area, had a very long hose, around 600 yards long. There were five plugs in the area, and in the event of a conflagration, the hose was taken to the nearest fireplug.

Despite many teething problems, for many residents of Govanhill and Crosshill, being independent remained a source of pride, and landlords particularly, had no desire to deal with the increased rates and regulations that they felt would come from being part of Glasgow. However, as the population of the two burghs grew, their finite resources were stretched to the limit and when new challenges emerged, they did not always cope with distinction. Outbreaks of infectious diseases like typhoid, occurred with regularity, fires were common, because many buildings were poorly constructed, and standards of safety were not as rigorous as they are now.

Incidents like these slowly turned the tide of opinion, and many became convinced that their fortunes would be improved if where they lived became part of Glasgow. For its part, Glasgow was eager to absorb the surrounding burghs into a new, larger municipality that it controlled. The city leaders complained of being *'cribbed, cabined confined'* by *'upstart burghs'*, which it argued correctly, in fact, were populated by many people who worked in Glasgow and enjoyed the services it provided, but because they lived just outside the city boundary made no contribution to that great expense, through the payment of rates.

One councillor argued that:

They are worthy burghs, every one of them, but they are neither self-created nor self-existent. They come

9

from the loins of Glasgow and they eat the bread which Glasgow gives them the means of earning. Yet they pretend to be independent, and they stand in the way of their great parent and tell her to her benignant face that she shall not extend her lines in their direction.

In 1885, a frustrated Glasgow Town Council successfully petitioned the Secretary of State for Scotland, and the Boundaries Commission were appointed to review Glasgow's relationship with its neighbouring burghs. In fact, the Boundaries Commission would make similar investigations around the country as other large municipalities sought to absorb smaller police burghs.

In 1887, the Commission finally recommended that Glasgow should be permitted the power to extend its current boundaries, subject to suitable negotiations with the neighbouring burghs. In 1889, the Extension of the City of Glasgow Act, was introduced in Parliament, not just in relation to Govanhill and Crosshill, but also to other burghs, like Govan and Partick.

Opinions were strongly divided within the burghs and in Parliament, and in November 1890, the bill failed at its second reading in the House of Lords, leading to celebrations on the streets of Govanhill.

A local journalist reported that:

The news flashed through the district like wildfire and steps were at once taken to celebrate the victory of the burghs by public rejoicing. The Third Renfrewshire Rifle Volunteers Brass Band from Thornliebank was engaged and arrived in the evening. Flags were hoisted at the Burgh Halls and at Victoria Cross, and the Govanhill Fire engine, drawn by two grey horses, paraded the burgh. A large bonfire containing over ten tons of wood, was built on vacant ground on Dixon Avenue and was lit at dusk, much to the delight of over one thousand of the juvenile population who occasionally indulged in a miniature display of fireworks. The band played in front of Provost Hunter's house and paraded the principal streets of the burgh until a late hour.

The celebrations were short-lived because the bill was resubmitted and passed in early 1891, but residents of the various burghs around Glasgow, still had to agree to annexation. In Govan, the idea of joining with Glasgow was simply dismissed out of hand. Crosshill voted by a clear majority to become part of Glasgow, the issue never really in doubt there, but opinions were more mixed in Govanhill. After Glasgow finally agreed to buy Dixon Halls, take

responsibility for several private streets and to build a new public park, the Govanhill councillors finally agreed to allow the issue of annexation to be put to a plebiscite. At the time, there were nearly 15,000 people living in Govanhill, yet despite the jubilant celebrations on the streets a few months earlier, only householders were eligible to vote. A total of 3,243 ballot papers were issued, only 2,404 were returned. One thousand and twenty-five votes were received in favour of annexation and 935 were opposed. By a majority of just 90 votes, the Burgh of Govanhill, which had been in existence for just 14 years, became, in November 1891, the 17th ward of the City of Glasgow.

The Govan Colliery and Dixon's Blazes

There is no doubt that two of the most significant enterprises in the history of Govanhill are the Govan Colliery and Govan Iron Works, widely known as Dixon's Blazes. These were more than just buildings, rather two industries that dominated the local landscape for nearly 200 years. Without them, Govanhill would have developed in a very different way. In their absence, we can only imagine how important they must have been to local people and the local economy.

The area that would become Govanhill, sitting just outside the City of Glasgow, would benefit greatly from the growth and expansion of the Industrial Revolution. There were great natural resources in the area waiting to be exploited and there was a laissez-faire attitude prevalent in society at the time, which allowed industry free reign, and entrepreneurs were not slow to seize the opportunity. One of those entrepreneurs was William Dixon (1753 – 1822) who came from Northumberland to manage the colliery and realised the potential in the area and laid the groundwork for further expansion. His son, also called William Dixon (1788 – 1859), built the Govan Iron Works and saw the business grow rapidly and his grandson William Smith Dixon (1824 – 1880) was directly responsible for the layout and construction of local streets and many important buildings, grand halls and tenements in Govanhill, many still standing to this day.

The Govan Colliery is first mentioned in records in 1717 but almost certainly there would have been some coal mining activity in the area for many years prior to that date. Thomas Richardson's 1795 map of the town of Glasgow and the country for seven miles around is the first to show the Govan Colliery or Coal Works, close to Bankhall House and situated approximately where modern-day Bankhall Street now stands. In the Statistical Account for Scotland in 1793, the Reverend William Anderson wrote:

The Govan Colliery has two excellent machines, the one for drawing up the water, the other a steam engine for bringing up coals 100 fathoms, which saves a number of horses. There are three seams of coal, the undermost 14 feet thick. It is thought that such a quantity of coals in the colliery as would of itself serve the city of Glasgow for 100 years to come.[1]

According to The Royal Commission on Coal Supply in 1871 it was estimated there were two billion tons of coal in the Clyde Valley of which 900 million tons were within 1,000 feet of the surface.

In the early 19th century, Govan Colliery was still a relatively small coal mining operation but would later come to occupy over 179 acres on the surface. There were several pits underneath modern-day Govanhill, many known just by a number. One pit that did have a name, however, was called the Allanton and was close to what is now Langside Road, part of which used to be called Allanton Terrace. In 1826, the Allanton Pit employed 13 miners, each producing 25 to 30 carts of coal per month.

The company houses that grew up around the colliery in the early 19th century became known as Fireworks Village, an early indication of the industrial activity that was beginning to transform the area. What would become Bankhall Street ran through the centre of the village. Other street and place names included Hosie's Land, Garden Square, Engine Row, Back Close, Carter Row, and Cuddy Row.

As the site developed, Fireworks would become larger and more cottages were built just north of the colliery, an outlier to the main village, between what is now Calder Street and Govanhill Street. In addition to the new cottages was a school, and the central street in this extension to Fireworks was called School Square.

School Square was still part of Govanhill in 1897, before being demolished to make way for new tenements. The colliery made money not just from coal but from renting houses to the miners and from ancillary businesses like pick-sharpening, selling horseshoes, scrap and even mine dust which would have useful mineral properties.

The 1841 census records 600 people living in Fireworks, two-thirds of them Irish, the rest mostly Scots. One hundred and sixty men were coal miners, there were 12 engine keepers, one hammerman, engineers, weighers and a joiner.

Robert Tancred, H.M. Inspector of Taxes, visited in 1842 when there were 808 people in the village. Women were prohibited from working in the pit but 49 of the 'men' in the pit were below the age of 13 with the working age at the time being just nine.

Tancred notes that one worker called Robert Ferguson was employed from 3.00am to 6.00pm. He was in charge of four drawers who would pull wagons to his shaft, three of those drawers were his brothers and the fourth was a boy who worked only for food and could remain in servitude to Ferguson *'all his days if he likes it'*.

Francis Connery, aged just nine years, was a trapper working from 6.00am to 6.00pm. Tancred reports:

He sits on a board in a niche in the wall without a light quite in the dark and holds a rope and so opens the door and when the carriage is passed, he shuts it again. He has some bread and tea sent down by the engine and brought to him by a drawer. Or if he should slack, he can run again and get it himself. It serves him for the day as long as he is down the pit.[2]

Before entering employment with the company, workers had to sign an agreement to obey certain company rules and two witnesses had to countersign this. Those rules included immediately vacating their house if they ceased employment, paying a certain amount of their wages back to the company for the necessities of life and, strangely, not keeping a dog.

New discoveries and techniques in the production of iron enabled a vast expansion of the business. In 1839, the Govan Iron Works were built just half a mile north of Fireworks Village. This new venture would become one of the most significant iron works in all of Scotland and would not only transform the area in and around Govanhill into a hive of industrial activity, but would arguably become one of the driving forces in the development of the new, emerging industrial city of Glasgow. By the early 1840s Govan Iron Works and Colliery were producing three times as much iron and coal as ever before.

Originally the new iron works had five blast furnaces, which would cast a bright glow for miles around and would become known as 'Dixon's Blazes'.

One commentator in 1849 said:

the bright glare cheers the long winter night and at the same time does the work of a score of policemen by scaring away the rogues and vagabonds who so plentifully infest other and darker parts of the city.

Many visitors to Glasgow were fooled by locals into thinking the suburbs were on fire and many local children were threatened with spending eternity in 'the bad fire' when they misbehaved.

The colliery needed to expand to fuel the new iron works and soon the site was active with foundries, boiler shops, a smithy, a turning shop, a fitting shop, a pattern shop, a moulding shop and coke ovens. There were also numerous railway lines transporting raw materials around the site and taking coal and many other finished goods offsite to other destinations. By 1856, the colliery was producing 11,517 carts of coal each year, 169 carts of ironstone and 28 carts of fire clay.

By the 1840s, engineering companies and many other industrial businesses were choosing to locate in the area to benefit from the close proximity of iron, coal and the many products that could be produced at Dixon's.

Fireworks Village was not sufficient anymore to house all of Dixon's employees, so in the late 1830s new company housing was built closer to the iron works. Some of this housing would become known as the Lower English Buildings. It may be true that many of the early workers came from England, particularly from Shropshire, as they had the skills and experience to work malleable iron that Scottish workers lacked. So, having accommodation on site would make the job of attracting new workers easier, particularly at times of industrial unrest, as a means of thwarting the strikers and breaking the strike.

The Lower English Buildings were single storey houses akin to cottages, with two main rooms divided up internally with box beds. Each house had a hearth and a range but running water had to be brought in from a standpipe outside in the yard. Recent archaeological excavations made during the construction of the M74 motorway revealed that the houses were surrounded by a number of small buildings used in different ways, as outhouses and washhouses, stables, a smithy, pigeon coops and even a kippering store.

Christina Wilson, born in the English Buildings in 1918, reflected on life there and recollected:

> You lit the fire on a Tuesday morning. The fire was going for the hot water and you crossed the whole lot of the yards with your rope to get your washing out. People couldn't live that way these days. My mother scrubbing from morning to night. They were good houses, not a thing wrong with them. We had a swee hanging on the fireplace, a kettle swee, a big iron kettle that hung on it. You had to polish it … you always had boiling water for tea … Oh aye … I liked my home.

Christina's niece, Jane Sutherland, recalls her aunt talking about slightly more difficult times, less coloured by nostalgia, when she had to *'fight to get washed'* in the morning and *'when everybody was in house, we'd have to sleep across the bed'*.

By the 1860s, the colliery was not exactly in decline but some seams of coal were running out which led to the less productive pits being closed and part of the colliery lands used for much-needed housing to accommodate workers at the rapidly expanding iron works. However, mining operations did continue at the Govan Colliery until the early 1900s. An inventory from 1900 documents not just all the tools, machinery and instruments required but horses above ground and below. Horses called Captain, Katy, Martin, Bob, Billy, Tommy and Peter worked above ground at No. 5 pit, while below ground wagons were pulled by Charley, Shark, Jock, Blyth, Daisy Bounce, Jimmy and Blackie.

Fireworks and the surrounding area was becoming more than just a village; the new houses and tenements being built to accommodate the growing population were transforming the area into a town and this expansion was of great interest to the neighbouring settlements. Crosshill to the south, already a well-established small town, wanted to expand its boundaries and claim the emerging population as its own. Glasgow, to the north, keen to expand its influence had in 1843, annexed the Burgh of Gorbals and wanted to expand further south.

Neither Crosshill nor Glasgow would succeed at this time in wooing the new town, which as a result became known as 'No Man's Land', a name that persisted until 1877 when the area was finally populous enough to qualify as an independent burgh and the name Govanhill was chosen.

William Dixon certainly encouraged this spirit of independence, not wanting his collieries or iron works to come under the influence of a municipal authority or to be obliged to pay municipal rates. He was also an absent landlord much of the time, mainly for reasons of health, and transformed Dixon's into a private limited company leaving much of the work to company trustees. This encouraged the idea that there was little or no authority in this nameless place.

Dixon passed away in 1880 but his empire, particularly the iron works, continued to thrive. In 1891, trade magazine *Commercial Glasgow* reported:

> The Govan Iron Works are a magnificent hive of busy industrial activity and an immense staff of employees is engaged in the various departments of the company's enterprise and it is gratifying to

record the prevalence of those cordial relationships between employers and employed which emphatically declare the liberality and consideration extended by great capitalists to a vast body of arduous toilers.

Regardless of the plight of the *'arduous toilers'*, Dixon's was no benevolent employer concerned for their workers' welfare like Robert Owen in New Lanark. Workers had to contend with back-breaking labour, dangerous levels of noise, environmental pollution and little official regard for safety. There were many accidents, often resulting in fatalities. *The Funeral Fund Roll Book* recorded every employee's marital status and the names of their dependants, if any. The first entry in the 1841 Roll Book is of a miner called James Allan born on 27th July 1795, with no dependants listed. Married men were first-class employees and single men were second-class employees. In the event of an accident, the families of married men would receive a contribution of two or three pounds for the loss of the family breadwinner, this amount varied depending on the number of dependants left behind. Second-class employees would get funeral costs covered. If an employee married, they could be reclassified as a first-class employee. Some notations next to the names of daughters or widows shows that they *'married out of the work'* rather than marrying another Dixon's employee.

By the end of the 19th century all accidents had to be logged by law, but despite the fact that some workers were now being trained as onsite 'ambulance workers' accidents were still commonplace.

In the same year that *Commercial Glasgow* praised the Dixon company's *'liberality and considerations towards its employees'* there was a strike over working conditions and pay. The furnaces were shut down during the strike and when they were eventually relit a tragic accident occurred:

THE SCOTSMAN Wednesday 11th March 1891

IRON WORKS EXPLOSION AT GLASGOW FIVE MEN KILLED AND INJURED

Yesterday forenoon, by an explosion which occurred at the ironworks of Messrs William Dixon (Limited), Cathcart Road, Glasgow, five men lost their lives and great damage was done to property. On the strike terminating a week ago, the works of Messrs Dixon again began to assume their former state of activity. There is always a certain danger attached to the relighting of furnaces, but this was proceeding satisfactorily when the explosion took place, entirely shattering one of the cylinder condensers or scrubbers. These chemical condensers are four in number, and are grouped together in a position to the northeast of the blast furnaces. Everything was prepared yesterday for the re-starting of the chemical apparatus, and a final examination was being made of the four condensers when about eleven o'clock a terrific explosion occurred in Number 4 scrubber. When the explosion took place, a huge volume of flame rose high in the air above the cylinders. The force of the explosion completely shattered the condenser, huge pieces of thick sheet iron having been thrown all over the works, great damage being done also to the houses in the surrounding district. Immediately after the occurrence the Glasgow Fire Brigade was called out, and it arrived under the charge of Captain Paterson and assisted in the rescue work. The rescue party had not laboured long before a lad named John Russell (18), employed as a labourer in the yard, was extricated from amongst the wreckage, his collar bone was broken and he was badly cut about the head, while his feet were also injured. He was removed to the Victoria Infirmary, having sufficient strength, as he was lifted into the wagon to make the request *'Don't tell mother'* to those around. As the bodies of the men found were taken out, they were conveyed to a store house fitted up as temporary mortuary and afterward removed to the houses of the deceased.

The following is a list of the dead. John S. Mullen (30) manager, married, residing at Dixon Avenue, Crosshill. Robert Guthrie, engineer (body not recovered). Robert McMillan (30) labourer, married, residing at Lower English Buildings Cathcart Road. Thomas Guthrie (35) engineer, unmarried residing at 31 Cathcart Road. Charles Dornan (43) engine fitter, married, residing at Hospital Street.

This tragic accident, just one of many and certainly not the worst, did little to significantly improve the situation for workers.

Gerald Fisher, whose father had a hairdressing business nearby with many of his customers working at Dixon's Blazes, recalled an early memory:

They were more or less crippled working there. The hot furnaces and then coming out into the cold – all sorts of rheumatism and what have you. Big heavy men, furnace men, steel workers, standing crippled at the corner.

In 1928, a worker by the name of John McCrindle was crushed to death when a wagon of ore was being shunted around the yard. The recently formed Accident and Prevention Committee issued the following advice:

> the committee is of the opinion that safety decisions are largely in the hands of the foreman and wish to impress upon the workforce the necessity for the exercise of judgement and caution.

In 1872, Govan Iron Works had become a private limited company, and the work was carried on by trustees. In 1906, it became a public limited company. In 1951, the company was nationalised and became part of the National Iron and Steel Corporation of Great Britain. In 1954 it was passed back to the private sector to a company called Colville's under a 'rationalisation' process.

The former owner, William Dixon, had expressed the hope in 1879 that, '... *the lights of the famous five blazes will grow ever brighter and continue to serve as one of the landmarks of Glasgow*', but a recession in 1958 meant that the furnaces were extinguished forever and hundreds of jobs were lost, a massive blow to the local economy.

The demolition, infilling of land and repurposing of the Dixon's site began in 1960. Taylor Woodrow bought a large part of the site to develop as an industrial estate and Templeton's Carpets bought 35 acres to build a new factory which opened in 1965. This factory closed in 1983 and was then followed by a cash and carry that would also close.

At the time of writing, many companies still operate on Dixon's Blazes Industrial Estate and new warehouses and retail outlets are being built.

Dübs & Company,
Polmadie North
British Locomotive Works

As in shipbuilding, Glasgow led the world in the design and construction of locomotives. Dübs and Company was a locomotive manufacturer based at the Queen's Park Works in Polmadie, at the very end of Calder Street. Founded by Henry Dübs, an engineer from Darmstadt in Germany, who had previously managed Beyer, Peacock and Company in Manchester and then the Neilson and Mitchell Locomotive Company in Finnieston. Dübs left Neilson's taking a number of key personnel with him to form his own rival company.

An article in the *Dundee Evening Post*, written in 1903, describes the location of the new business, simply known as the Queen's Park Locomotive works:

> There was no Polmadie as now we know it. The works were situated in the midst of green fields and the cry of the corncrake and twittering notes of the starling and blackbird blended with the striking of hammers and the hum of machinery in motion.

The first train produced by Dübs, rolled off the production line in early 1865, the new business grew quickly and soon rivalled Neilson's and other competitors. Records from 1865 show the inventory was already worth over £42,000.

Early salary books show that the workforce tripled in the first three years. Notably, on 25th August 1866, the first mention is made of three female tracers; Miss Annie Hay, Mary Brownlie and Lydia Robertson, each earning six shillings per week. Dübs insisted that women would be better tracers (and perhaps conveniently could be paid less) but men and women were strictly segregated in the workplace and even one hundred years later, fraternisation of male and female workers was frowned upon.

When Dübs died in 1867, the company continued to prosper and by 1871 employed over 1,000 people, were building over 100 locomotives per year and the expanded site occupied over eight and a half acres. A new locomotive crane was invented and patented by Dübs & Co. and they were soon building over 200 of them per year, in addition to locomotives.

Order books show that the first locomotives built at Polmadie were for export to Europe, Russia, New Zealand and China, costing anywhere from £4,000 to £12,000. One of the 508 series was sold to Imperial Russia, at a cost of £5,862 for the carriage and £1,954 for the engine. Freight to Saint Petersburg cost £512, insurance £952, expenses £93 and the cost of erecting £179. Gradually orders came in for the domestic market as well, many for Scottish railways such as the Glasgow and South Western Railway Company, which ran trains south to Ayrshire.

Situated close to the Govan Iron Works, Dübs was a hot and busy place to work, leading to the workers composing this song:

> *We're railway men at Polmadie*
> *In a hotter place you couldn'a be*
> *And when in Hell we gather when we dee*
> *We'll be nane the waur than in Polmadie!*

On 1st April 1903, Dübs had 2,500 employees on a 24-acre site. The same year, they merged with former rivals the Atlas Works and the Hyde Park Works from Springburn to form the North British Locomotive Company which would become the largest locomotive engineering company in Europe and were dubbed by many journalists as *'pioneers of the iron road'*.

The combined workforce numbered over 8,000 people with the capacity to build over 600 locomotives per year and the site at Polmadie was extended, more than doubling in size.

The trademark of the new company was based on the diamond shape used by Dübs, which in turn was taken from the logo of the Govan Brick Works, situated near the Govan Colliery.

In 1914, as well as producing trains, they made shells and sea mines for the war effort. By 1920, they had made over 22,000 locomotives for customers around the world. That was also their best year on record with profits of over £1,000,000.

In 1927, after completing an order for 50 locomotives of the Royal Scot type for the London, Midland and Scottish Railway Company, the *Glasgow Evening News* said *'these locomotives are the last word in engineering, ingenuity and skill'*. In 1935, the three factories produced 21,300 locomotives.

An early promotional article in trade magazine British Industries, Issue 10 in 1905, described operations at Queen's Park:

After the designer has thought about his engine, he can test the working of moving parts by means of a large model fixed to the wall of the designing room. In this large model he can lengthen or shorten the cranks and levers to agree with his drawing and by watching the valves he can see the results.

Being assured that everything is quite alright then drawings go to the tracing room where a number of young lady artists make careful tracings of them and those tracings are used as negatives for obtaining photographic blueprints. To make these prints a large upright cylinder is used, within which, there travels automatically up and down a powerful electric lamp while tracing with the sensitised paper beneath it makes a journey around the cylinder, taking about a minute to do the work.

Some of these blueprints go to the pattern makers who constructed wooden patterns to enable the moulders to form the sand moulds for the casting of iron and brass and other prints go to the shop where templates are made.

These latter are really patterns of substantial sheet iron carefully drilled to show where holes are to be made in the actual working. The template of the frame is really an exact pattern of what the actual thing is to be.

As everyone travels in a train nowadays, it was a matter of considerable interest to learn the care taken in the selection of proper material by the North British locomotive company and in this respect, they represent all the leading locomotive makers in the world to ensure travelling shall be safe.

It was always a memorable day in Polmadie and Govanhill, when a train was being transported through the streets to the River Clyde for shipping overseas.

The trade slump of the 1920s and 1930s hit the company hard but there was a brief upturn in orders after World War Two. By 1950, the drawing office in Polmadie had over 100 draughtsmen and 50 female tracers but the age of steam was almost over.

After the British Railways Modernisation Act of 1955, the company was forced to undergo a major reorganisation in order to build new diesel, electric and hydroelectric trains, but their efforts were found wanting. The decision to make locomotives with hydraulic rather than electric transmission proved flawed. Trains were regularly returned for repair and previously loyal customers drifted away. Other companies had made the necessary adjustments earlier and more successfully. Combined with too much reliance on the overseas market, the company began to lose orders.

The Queen's Park Works closed in 1962 with the loss of over 1,000 jobs.

The Sentinel Works
Alley and McLellan

Alley and McLellan was a mechanical engineering company based on Jessie Street in Polmadie, founded by Irishman Stephen Alley and Glaswegian John McLellan. The company began by building engines, valves, compressors, cranes and other parts for trains and steamships using the brand name Sentinel.

Originally based in Bridgeton, they moved to Polmadie in 1880 in search of larger premises and were soon employing nearly 1,000 men on a ten-acre site. Polmadie was sparsely populated but the land they had acquired was intersected by the Caledonian Railway and also conveniently close to Dixon's Iron Works, so they enjoyed good transport links and easy access to raw materials. The company also secured options for more land in the area and within five years the Polmadie site had doubled in size.

With more space and greater capacity, they began building complete ships, despite being far from the Clyde. They specialised in passenger steamers, tug boats, barges, and a variety of craft capable of carrying heavy cargo in shallow water.

William S. Murphy's book, *Captains of Industry* from 1891, tells us *'... there is a shipbuilding yard in Glasgow from which never a ship is launched but where many a ship is built'*.

All the ships built in Jessie Street were assembled using nuts and bolts, then dismantled and shipped in crates to their destination where they were reassembled using rivets. Parts smaller than four feet in length could be packed in crates but larger parts were drawn to the docks by horses. Inland lakes such as Lake Baikul in Russia or parts of the River Nile could now be navigated by ships built in Polmadie. By 1899, Alley and McLellan had built over 200 steamers and total output measured over two million tons. Clients included the War Office, the British Navy, the India Office and the Colonial Office.

One Alley and McLellan ship still in service in the early 1990s was the SS Chauncy Maples. Chauncy Maples was an Anglican missionary serving in Africa who drowned when his boat capsized on his way to take up his duties in 1895. All 18 African men and boys on board swam to safety but Maples drowned because of the weight of his cassock.

The ship was commissioned by the Oxford and Cambridge Universities Mission to Central Africa in 1899 and completed in 1901 for a cost of £13,500.

The SS Chauncy Maples was then disassembled into 3,500 packages. A special train carriage was constructed to move the nine-and-a-half-ton boiler and 150 hefty Glaswegians hauled the carriage to the docks with ropes. Transport to Africa cost £5,500 and then 450 Angoni tribesmen pulled the carriage and boiler over 100 miles to the lake, covering about three miles per day.

The Chauncy Maples served honourably as a hospital ship for a number of years but has been laid up since 1992 awaiting restoration and its fate currently remains uncertain.

In the first half of the 20th century, the shipbuilding operation declined, but Alley and McLellan became known for the Sentinel Steam Waggon which was conceived of as a cheaper alternative to the horse and cart. The double 'g' in Waggon was deliberate, a marketing ploy to set the

Sentinel apart from other vehicles. Although much noisier, it could pull heavier loads.

The Sentinel was so successful that a new factory was built in Shrewsbury to deal with orders. After just a few years, petrol lorries eventually proved more economical, and new vehicle licensing charges introduced in the 1930s favoured petrol lorries.

Many Sentinel Waggons continued to serve a purpose until the late 1950s, but like the steam engine they too were overtaken and replaced by diesel and electric engines. When production of the Steam Waggon was moved to Shrewsbury, the factory at Polmadie concentrated on making air and gas compressors which powered turbines of all kinds in collieries, shipyards, quarries, gold mines, railway depots, and even on foghorns around the coast. The Polmadie factory also had a foundry which produced iron castings for marine and heavy engineering.

Alley and McLellan continued to operate at the Sentinel Works in Jessie Street until the 1950s producing various engineering products. Eventually they became a subsidiary of a larger company, called Glenfield and Kennedy, and operations moved to Kilmarnock. The company finally dissolved in 1975, while the Sentinel Works were used by a number of smaller engineering companies until the 1970s.

As of 2021, the Sentinel Works remains standing in Jessie Street but has been in a derelict condition for a long time. The most distinctive part of the works, the design and patent office built in 1903, was the first steel-reinforced concrete building in Scotland and as such is listed as category A, signifying it is a building of national importance.

Now there is a car boot sale on the Sentinel site each week.

Larkfield Omnibus Depot

The Glasgow Tramway Act was enacted by Parliament in 1870. In 1872, a private company, the Glasgow Tramway and Omnibus Company, laid a two-and-a-half-mile track from St George's Cross to Eglinton Toll, via Sauchiehall Street and Victoria Bridge, and was granted a 22-year lease to run horse-drawn trams on the route. The line could not go any further because Eglinton Toll was at that time the city boundary.

As the city expanded over the next few years, more lines were added around the city and the first line to Eglinton Toll was extended south to Crosshill in 1877, terminating at Queen's Park.

Glasgow's tramlines had an unusual track gauge which allowed railway wagons to be drawn along tramway streets to access some shipyards. Glasgow Corporation declined to renew Glasgow Tramway's lease in 1894 and instead took the tramlines into municipal ownership and formed Glasgow Corporation Tramways.

Electrification of the tramlines began in 1898 and by 1902 the horse-drawn tramway service was withdrawn. At the same time, motor buses began to make an appearance on the roads of most cities, many operated by private companies, but in Glasgow trams would remain the dominant form of transport for many years to come. The Corporation eventually became responsible for both trams and motor buses.

By the 1920s, opinion was divided on whether trams or motor buses were the most efficient form of transport. Buses were becoming faster and could make journeys that trams could not, but trams still covered the majority of routes around the city. Many Glaswegians came to rely on the two forms of public transport and the subsidised fares.

In 1894, 1.1 million journeys were taken on trams but by 1930, 10.3 million tram and motor bus journeys were made. Over this period of expansion, many people took jobs with Glasgow Corporation Tramways; in 1894 the company employed 927 people but by 1930 there were 8,624 employees.

In 1929, the Corporation built its first omnibus depot on the Larkfield estate on Butterbiggins Road. At the time, the depot was the largest of its kind in the UK with space for over 100 buses. This was deemed necessary to accommodate the extra buses required to compete with private companies.

The original plans for Larkfield show that in 1929, Old Langside Road still ran through the centre of the estate, a private road leading to Larkfield House. Inglefield House and Butterbiggins Cottage can also be seen on the plans, but before the new garage was built all of those houses were demolished.

Shortly after this, the Corporation was also granted a monopoly on public transport for most of the city, so that a further extension to the Larkfield depot was then required.

In 1931, the garage was extended, creating room for 160 buses, making it again the largest and best equipped omnibus depot in Britain, with all the necessary facilities to service the fleet. Plans were even made to lay down a greasy track on which drivers could be taught to correct skidding, previously practised on quiet, open roads.

Over half of Glasgow's omnibuses were now based at Larkfield.

The interior of the depot was well-equipped including, a hot water circulating system, fans to circulate fresh air via ducts throughout the building, underground storage with space for 3,500 gallons of fuel oil, ten gallons of engine oil and 300 gallons of paraffin oil. There was also a large portable vacuum to clean upholstery, a washing bay and a paint shop with space to work on three buses at the same time.

By 1936, Larkfield was no longer the largest depot in Glasgow but in many ways remained the most important because all buses in the fleet were sent there for servicing or 'dock overhaul' after completing 25,000 miles.

During World War Two, many women were recruited for machine shop jobs in Larkfield, though some relinquished those jobs when the men returned from serving overseas. There was also a Home Guard unit operating out of Larkfield. There must have been plenty of room for drilling in the depot and they practised manoeuvres in the by-then derelict workers' cottages known as the 'English Village' close to Govan Iron Works.

Buses and trams continued to operate on the streets of Glasgow until 1962, when the trams were finally taken out of service. (Some of Glasgow's trams were transported to Hong Kong, where they continued in service for many years. Although the fleet has since been modernised, some old trams are still retained for their heritage value, and tourists can still ride on them, on certain routes.)

Many more buses were now required on the routes previously covered by trams, so a further extension of the Larkfield depot was required to deal with the vastly increased fleet. When the extension was completed in 1964, Larkfield could accommodate 266 buses and there was even space to build buses as the nearby Coplawhill depot was in the process of being closed down.

In May 1992, a devastating fire destroyed much of the extension built in 1964 and 60 buses were lost, each valued at £100,000, meaning the financial loss was over £6,000,000. Buses were quickly purchased from other cities and for months afterwards many different liveries could be seen around Glasgow.

Larkfield continued to function until 2014 but long before that it was obvious that the depot was past its best, and a new modern facility was required. On 18th October 2014, Larkfield closed its doors for the last time and operations moved to the new Caledonia Depot just a short distance away, built on the site of the old Southside Railway Station.

The depot at Larkfield has now been demolished and, at the time of writing, under partnership between Glasgow City Council and Link Housing, many new mid-market houses have been constructed, 150 new homes are planned in total.

Govanhill Baths and The Steamie

As the population of Glasgow grew and the city expanded throughout the 19th century, there was little scope for respite from the smoke, grime and overcrowding that pervaded so many aspects of industrial life. With no formal facilities for swimming, rivers were the only option for the working classes to enjoy this popular and free pastime. Despite the obvious dangers and without any formal instruction, people swam to wash away the dirt of the working week and to enjoy a little recreation. Inevitably, accidents happened and many drowned. The Glasgow Humane Society was formed in 1790 to help people in difficulties on the river and unfortunately to recover corpses. In addition, for many people, the rivers of Glasgow were the only place to wash their clothes.

In 1869, Glasgow Corporation's Sanitary Committee, keen to address these issues, called for the building of baths and washhouses around the city. However, beyond the freeing up of land for the building of some private swimming pools, little happened in that decade. In 1875, they returned to the issue and formed the Baths and Washhouses Committee, who were charged with building four new municipal facilities at key points around the city. There had been a private washhouse on Glasgow Green since the early 18th century but that building and the land were acquired in order to begin this great municipal enterprise and so Greenhead Baths and Washhouses opened three years later in 1878.

An open-air pool was built in Alexandra Park in 1877 and temporary swimming pools opened on London Road and Kennedy Street in the same year, to test the demand and the popularity, but closed in 1883 when the other 'roofed-in' facilities began to open.

When Greenhead opened, Govanhill was not yet part of the city of Glasgow. The Victoria Baths, opened in 1877 on Butterbiggins Road, which was at that time part of the Burgh of Gorbals and thus part of the municipality of Glasgow, did provide swimming for some well-heeled residents, but as a private members club access was beyond the reach of most working people.

As for washing clothes and bedding, no doubt there were some small backcourt washhouses behind the tenements or cottages that existed at the time, and some private laundry facilities for those who could afford the cost, but for most people opportunities were limited. Washing clothes in the tub at home would be common for many at this time but in small, overcrowded flats this would inevitably cause some domestic disharmony.

Govanhill finally became part of Glasgow in 1891 but it took until 1912 before plans were made to build a baths and washhouse in the area. Work started in 1914 to build the new facility and washhouse on an empty Corporation site on Calder Street.

The foundation stone was laid by Provost Daniel Stevenson on 4th of July 1914, just after Councillors Drummond and Sloan had placed a casket containing, according to the *Glasgow Herald*, '*documents etc*', in a cavity, and then the foundation stone was put in place and the assembled crowd sang the 100th Psalm.

The outbreak of war a few weeks later significantly delayed construction, during which time many citizens complained about the reckless expenditure of ratepayers' money, predicting the costs would exceed the Corporation's estimates of £45,000. The final costs were £40,000 for the baths, £35,000 for the washhouse or steamie, and £5,182 and ten shillings for the land, leased by the Baths and Washhouse Committee from the Corporation. Many continued to raise concerns about the cost of running all the baths around the city; none of them were hugely profitable but many in the Corporation were firmly committed to the idea that the health and social benefits would outweigh the financial costs.

Govanhill Baths finally opened on 28th February 1917 and Provost Thomas Dunlop proudly proclaimed '*the inhabitants of Glasgow were highly favoured in having in their midst the best equipped baths in Glasgow*'.[4] A journalist writing in the *Daily Record* described the baths as '*palatial*' and wrote, '*the whole pile is really the last word in baths, public and private, there is nothing finer anywhere in the kingdom*'.[5]

The opening ceremony at Govanhill included '*a graceful display of swimming*' by two champion women swimmers, Mary Strathearn and Bella Moore, holder of all Scottish records at the time.

The *Glasgow Herald* described the new baths in great detail:

The site of the baths is on ground belonging to the Corporation at Calder and Kingarth Street and covers an area of 3455 square yards. The frontages to those walls are built of stone and the others of brick. The walls inside are tiled; the floors of bath and pond rooms are of terrazzo and the floors of the hot room are of tile. There are two swimming ponds and a 'learners' pond with hot and cold sprays, foot baths etc. in each pond room; a Turkish bath with three hot rooms, a Russian bath, a shampooing room with two marble slabs, a cold plunge baths, a cooling-room with 20 beds etc. the water in the ponds is heated by the exhaust steam from a pump which is used for drawing the water continuously from the ponds, and is worked in connection with the filtration and aeration plant. There is an arrangement for mixing salt connected with this plant so that salt water baths can be had. The ponds do not require to be emptied except for repairs. Ferro-concrete has been extensively used in the construction of the buildings. The public washhouse enters from Kingarth Street. It is fitted with 68 wash stalls and space has been reserved for another 14. Drying accommodation is provided for each stall and there are ten wringing machines. A large waiting room is provided at the entrance from Kingarth Street.

The *Daily Record* provided a brief description of the building but did also mention *'twenty first-class and twenty second-class slipper baths for males on the first floor'* and *'11 slipper baths for females'*.

In the first months of opening, from March to August 1917, 160,000 people availed themselves of the palatial new facility on their doorstep, more than any other public baths. A swim cost just 2d for adults and 1d for children and included a hot spray. If the ponds were closed, hot baths were available for 3d but it was obviously better value to get a hot spray and a swim. Eighty thousand men and 40,000 women came to swim, and 30,000 people came for hot baths. The facilities available in the washhouse cost 3d per hour with most women booking two hours at a time.

In 1917, the pools and baths were strictly gender segregated; what is now known as the main pool was originally called the men's pond and the smaller of the two main pools was called the women's pond. Even the entrance to the building itself was segregated; the doors nearest to Victoria Road were the men's entrance and the doors closer to the centre of the building were the women's entrance. Hooks on the walls outside held signs designating the different entrances, which can still be seen today. In the foyer, there was even a ticket kiosk keeping men and women apart.

By October of 1917, the City Lighting Authorities, perhaps for financial reasons or in anticipation of a cold winter (the winter of 1916 had been considerably colder than the average) insisted on the baths closing at 5.30pm. Attendance figures were beginning to decline, perhaps because so many men were serving overseas in the war effort, but this reduction in service led to many complaints and many letters to the newspapers demanding longer opening hours be resumed.

One correspondent calling herself *'A Munition Girl'* asked, *'What are we working girls to do as evening is our only time for recreation?'*, and concluded with *'If the baths only remained open until 7 or 7.30pm it would give working girls a fair chance'*. After many letters, the authorities relented and late opening was re-established by November.

Not everyone was happy though, and there were many complaints about the temperature and cleanliness of the water. The chimney above the baths was also a cause of concern. One concerned citizen using the pseudonym *'Indignant Householder'* complained of the black smoke being *'emitted incessantly'* from the chimney at Calder Street while *'Disgusted'* added the smoke *'would do credit to a destroyer flotilla'*.

In the early 1920s, filtration methods improved dramatically, which would certainly have improved the swimming experience, and mixed swimming was permitted from 1920, prompting one concerned citizen to write a letter to the *Daily Record*:

> Sir, in my opinion mixed bathing is not only shockingly immoral but tends to degenerate especially among the female sex. If a girl who was a party to such an indulgence, attempted to win me over by her affections with a view to partnership I would very quickly inform her that I would prefer a girl with some degree of womanliness and self-respect.
>
> I would ask two questions. Is mixed bathing necessary and why is this system being instituted?
>
> Private Bather.

However popular swimming was, prices were kept low to encourage people to use the amenities. The Corporation would supplement its income by occasionally hiring the pools out to churches for baptisms. In June 1928, Pastor Gilbert T. Fletcher of the Bible Standard Free Church came to Govanhill Baths to baptise more than 160 people. The pastor wore a waterproof jacket, trousers and galoshes and entered the pool at the shallow end. Those receiving baptism, mostly women and children, wore suits of heavy material and the women wore caps. The 'dippings' involved total immersion under the water.

After the ceremony, the pastor invited anyone from the congregation who wished to be baptised to come down into the pool. On this occasion, more than six people volunteered.

The washhouse, or steamie as it was commonly known, was a working space, frequented exclusively by women, so there is much less recorded material available for research. What few documents, newspaper articles and photographs that survive are hard to locate but some gems can still be located.

Looking at the broader story of the development of the washhouses gives some indication of their importance and the impact they had on working lives.

In 1916, Arthur Sowray, a leading advocate for the establishment of washhouses, described how for typical households and families without access to a public washhouse, wash-day, which could last three or four days, was similar to having a spring clean every single week.

It would often start on Monday morning when dirty clothes had to be collected and put into steep. If it was a wet day, the husband of the house would arrive home to find tea not ready and wet clothes hanging in front of the fire and across the living room on cords. *'All home comfort is gone, with the result that the husband is driven out to the nearest pub or club for the night, to get what comfort he can elsewhere'.*[6]

On the Wednesday, if the clothes were sufficiently dried off, they would be folded ready for mangling. The husband, if he was at home, would have the dubious *'pleasure'* of turning the mangle after a hard day's work. Thursdays were reserved for ironing and final airing of the clothes and on Friday the clothes would be put away. Sowray argued that if public washhouses were used, all the family's clothes and bedding could be washed and dried in just a few hours.

For many around Glasgow, it seemed, on certain days of the week at least, that the whole life of the neighbourhood revolved around the washhouse.

Numerous reports talk about how the smell of soap was everywhere in a typical steamie. Clouds of steam would rise up from the tubs and machines that were always in demand.

In its own way, the work at the steamie was just as physically demanding as work done by men in a factory or shipyard. Many women suffered rheumatic pain induced in part by hours spent hunching over a washtub while standing in water. Many would work barefoot to save shoe leather; others would wear wellington boots or their husband's old work boots.

Despite the heat and the dampness and the heavy work involved, the social life of the steamie was memorable for many women, a chance to meet friends and share news and gossip, a welcome relief from the busy life of running a family and a household and maybe even holding down a part-time job.

In Scotland, until the 1950s, the New Year was a more significant holiday than Christmas. Steamies would open early and shut late during Christmas week, so that the house was perfectly clean for any first-footers who would arrive on Hogmanay or early in January.

In 1954, *Daily Record* reporter Donald Bruce came to Govanhill not to write about women heroically washing clothes but to report on the social life of the women who frequented *'the big place'* on Calder Street.

It all began when one of the regulars at the steamie, Mrs Janet Wilson of 63 Aikenhead Road, heard that Jean McFarlane, one of the office staff, was leaving. Mrs Wilson organised a leaving party at a small hall just off nearby Allison Street. The event was only for Jean and the women who worked at the steamie and men were not allowed or invited.

The event was so popular that one of the party goers suggested they should meet regularly and so the idea of 'The Steamie Ball' was born and became a fortnightly event. The women would meet, dance and 'have a tare'.

The only men who were allowed to attend were the band and the MC, who had to perform as well as preside over events.

In the 1960s, washing machines were becoming more commonplace but many women could not afford one, or resisted staying at home to do their washing, preferring the camaraderie of the washhouse. However, the Corporation had to move with the times, upgrade machinery and offer a new level of service. So, in 1973, the Govanhill washhouse became more like a laundrette.

The letter below from the Corporation of Glasgow Baths to local councillor James O'Sullivan outlined the new changes:

From Corporation of Glasgow Baths

To Councillor J. O'Sullivan

Govanhill Baths

The modernization of the washhouse is well underway after an initial set back caused by the builders strike last year. The new washing machines, tumble-driers, hydro-extractors and ironing machines have now been delivered and placed in position and it now remains to connect water, power, steam etc.

In the meantime, the existing machines are working as usual and there is no interference with the service but when we come to finish the floor at the entrance then the washhouse will have to be closed for perhaps two weeks.

The new machinery will be modern and compact and will be accommodated in the area of existing washhouse. This will give the new washhouse the appearance of a laundrette and the customers will not have such great distances to walk between the washing machines and dryers. New stainless-steel sinks are being installed and they will be hidden away in a separate area so that the main floor can be kept dry.

When the new machines are in operation, we will fit a false ceiling with concealed lighting and cover the old glazed brick with wood panelling and other finishes to give the place a more pleasing appearance.

The new machines should be in operation by the beginning of May on the building, operation and decoration completed sometime in August.

Yours faithfully
James Russell
General manager 1973

An article in *Southside News* in 1975, revealed that while some aspects of the changes were welcomed, the loss of the booking system dryers which could be reserved was lamented. Those vintage dryers, which had been in operation since 1917, were used mainly for drying woollen items and heavy fibreglass laden curtains which could not be put into the newer dryers:

At the Govanhill steamie in Kingarth Street, which was modernised about three years ago, Mrs Margaret Toye of 93 Prince Edward Street has been waiting for a machine for an hour. She does three washings a week and says the average waiting time is an hour.

Mrs Toye has been using Govanhill washhouse for 30 years, first with her mother, now in her own right.

Says Margaret 'the new machines only take about half the washing and have been moved to the back of the building. That really is an improvement. You're not ploughing through water all the time. And with these new machines you don't get soaked when you're taking the washing out it's almost dry'.

Mangles and folding tables have been retained and of course they've got the easy chairs but says

Mrs Toye 'You don't get as good a wash; you can't with only 20 minutes, but it's still better than the launderettes. I preferred the booking system. The kids still aren't allowed in so it means you have to leave them in the waiting room. It didn't use to suit everyone though it was more for the housewives. Now it stays open later. The last wash used to be 5 o'clock which wasn't much use for working people. Now it's 8pm most days. A lot of people who used to have to go to the commercial laundrette now come here'.

The washhouse finally closed in 1990. In 2001, despite local opposition culminating in a five-and-a-half-month occupation of the building which was forcefully ended by the police and the council, the baths finally closed after 82 years of service to the community.

The activists who had led the occupation formed Govanhill Baths Community Trust and the campaign to save the baths continued, aided by the listing of the building by Historic Scotland, which prevented demolition.

It took time for the council to listen to the concerns of locals and by 2010 the baths had been derelict for nearly ten years. A small grant from the Scottish Government allowed a partial reopening in 2012.

The pools were not able to be opened but the rooms at the front of the building were converted to offices, a community kitchen and spaces available for local groups to hire. The steamie became an impromptu theatre and cinema space. Between 2012 and 2018, led by Govanhill Baths Community Trust, many local groups found a home and a space for their activities and events, and many local people found the help, advice and social space they desperately needed. Between 2016 and 2018, the small learners' pool had a limited opening to allow infants to learn to swim.

In 2019, funding was finally secured for a major redevelopment of the building and at the time of writing, the building has been closed again temporarily to prepare for the renovation. It is scheduled to reopen in 2023, with two functioning swimming pools, a gym, event space and useful spaces and rooms to serve the needs of the local community.

In the 20th century, the Govanhill Baths and Washhouse served a particular purpose, to provide hygienic washing facilities and a space to enjoy the healthy pursuit of swimming.

The new, reinvigorated and repurposed building will serve a very similar purpose for the 21st century. It will not only provide swimming but will also cater in multiple ways for the health and wellbeing of local people.

The Royal Samaritan Hospital for Women

In 1885, the Glasgow Samaritan Hospital for Women opened on Cumberland Street. Led by Dr Stuart Nairne, who had recently founded the Glasgow Obstetrical and Gynaecological Society, this was an effort to replicate the work of the famous Samaritan Free Hospital in London. In spite of objections from the Samaritan Society based at the Western Infirmary, who did not want their subscribers confused, they refused to change the name.

The governors of the new hospital sought to alleviate the:

...widespread and for the most part hidden sufferings of women among the respectable poor afflicted, through no fault of their own, with diseases incident to their sex which rendered their lives a burden to themselves and involved their homes and families in far reaching misery and neglect.

And to provide:

...rest, quietness, special nursing and watchful care which a hospital reserved for themselves can of necessity best bestow.

The new hospital had three main objectives:

1. The provision of medical and surgical treatment for women suffering from diseases peculiar to their sex. It was also felt that smaller wards would be more conducive to recovery.

2. The promotion of research and instruction of students.

3. Training of women's nurses.

The Cumberland Street Hospital was an immediate success but only had three beds, a small clinic and dispensary. By 1890, it was clear that larger premises were required and an appeal was launched to raise funds. This move took not the anticipated two years to complete but nearly six years. While plans were being laid and new ground sought, temporary new premises were acquired at Kingston House in St. James Street, near what now forms part of the approach to the Kingston Bridge.

The fundraising target was £5,000. Glasgow's titled ladies came to the fore and formed the Ladies Auxiliary Association, who would play a significant role in the development of the Hospital for the next 60 years. The association decided to hold a Bazaar in St. Andrews Halls from 27th to 29th of November 1890. Events like this were not unknown but the ladies of the association took the idea to a new level. Attractions included: fortune telling from the Romany Queen, a fish pond, an orchestra, organ recitals, waxworks, and a demonstration of Edison's Phonograph, which was described in the programme as *'the talking machine that is a wonder the world'*.

Patrons at the Bazaar were encouraged to participate or buy items at the different stalls. A poem entitled *Our Bazaar* in the programme gave a helpful guide and enticed them to spend their money. The first few verses went so:

Come Haste to St Andrews Hall
Where is held our Grand Bazaar
With its bright and beautiful stalls
Richly stored with wares from afar

There are maidens blooming and fair
All eager to serve and to sell
And Gypsy sirens are there
Awaiting your fortune to tell

And flower girls, in gold and white
Are tripping with flowers through the hall
While matrons beaming and bright
Are presiding, with grace, over all

And the last verse urged guests not to delay:

Then haste if you wish to buy
For the bargains are going fast
And to fully avail of the three days sale
You must not be the last

The Bazaar ended up raising £5,300. Eventually, land owned by Glasgow Corporation on Coplaw Street was acquired, after the board of Governors persuaded the Corporation to reduce their asking price by one third. The architectural firm of McWhannell and Rogerson, well known as *'careful and good architects'* were appointed to design the new hospital.

The foundation stone was laid in May 1895 and the opening ceremony took place a few months later on 9th September 1896.

The total cost of construction was £16,000. Much of the remaining balance had been raised from donations and private subscriptions. Subscribers got the chance to endow a bed or even nominate patients for treatment. Ten years after the original hospital had opened, they now had new, permanent facilities and capacity for 30 beds. In those first years, 1,600 patients were treated annually at a cost of £2,400, raised entirely by voluntary contributions.

The opportunity to rest in pleasant surroundings with a high standard of care would undoubtedly have led to a swifter recovery and must have been a source of delight to dwellers from the tenements. There may have been less privacy than the Cumberland Street Hospital but the Ladies Auxiliary Association, and an offshoot organisation called The Dorcas Society, helped create a comfortable environment by providing furnishings and spectacular displays of flowers throughout the hospital. There were pianos in every ward and each Monday afternoon there was a pianoforte or violin recital, songs and *other pleasant entertainments*. In an age before radio or television, such efforts would have surely been welcomed.

The new hospital was only a fraction of the size that it would become but the governors had the foresight to acquire enough land for future expansion. One year before the opening, in 1895, one of the governors, J. K. Kelly, wrote a letter to the board urging them to buy land closer to Victoria Road in order to have space in the future for various aims including teaching opportunities, to be a maternity hospital, to be part of a future south side medical school and a possible Women's College of Medicine. All of those predictions would come true, in one way or another.

In 1900, for the first time, two women directors were appointed to the board. In 1902, costs were rising, the waiting list was four times larger than capacity and it was clear that a new wing was required. An appeal went out for £15,000 and largely increased contributions. The Ladies Auxiliary Association came to the fore again, proceeds from the 1903 Bazaar raised £25,000 and enabled the building of a new wing, completed in 1907, and an increase of capacity to 48 beds.

In 1903, Mrs Polson, the President of the Ladies Auxiliary Association, whose fortune came from the Brown and Polson wheat manufacturing company, lost her daughter and so gifted to the hospital the money to build a nurse's home which would become known as the Alice Mary Corbett Memorial Nurses Home. The foundation stone was laid on 27th October 1904 by the Honourable Godfrey Corbett, the donor's grandson, and formally opened by Mrs Polson herself on 12th April 1906. Soon after, nurses began to reside at the hospital and principal nurse Mrs Maitland was made resident matron.

By 1907, with the opening of the new wing, the Glasgow Samaritan Hospital for Women was now the largest gynaecological hospital in the United Kingdom.

In recognition of this success, King Edward VII, who had been patron of the hospital while Prince of Wales, granted the use of the term Royal in renaming the hospital, now known henceforth as the Royal Samaritan Hospital for Women.

In 1912, further expansion was required but by now other hospitals were replicating the fundraising methods employed by the Ladies Auxiliaries, ruling out any new bazaar for the Royal Samaritan in 1912 and 1913. The outbreak of war in 1914 delayed the process indefinitely. The war came to an end four years later but it took until 1921 before a sense of normality was restored and the question of expansion could be considered again. However, other hospitals had already indicated their intention to hold bazaars in 1922 and 1923, so a date in November 1924 was booked.

The target amount to be raised this time was £70,000. The bazaar, again in St. Andrews' Hall, was very similar in style to the first bazaar in 1890 with Gypsy fortune-telling and various activities such as fishing, Wheel of Fortune, Hoopla and a Bool Race.

In the programme, a poem entitled *The Building of The Wing* laid out the challenge and encouraged people to contribute:

> *The Chairman of the Hospital*
> *By the nine gods he swore*
> *That the famous 'Royal Samaritan'*
> *Should be enlarged once more*
> *By the nine Gods he swore it.*
> *Then lustily called he:*
> *'Come hither, good McWhannell*
> *And draw the plans for me.'*
>
> *The Architect then sat him down,*
> *And Laboured Day and Night,*
> *The difficulties in the way*
> *Might many a man a-fright;*
> *And new demands came rushing in,*
> *Whichever way you look,*
> *Such as 'More rooms for nurses,'*
> *And 'A better place to cook'*
>
> *But the Chairman's brow was sad,*
> *And the Chairman's speech was low*
> *When he learned how much it would all cost –*
> *Seventy thousand pounds or so.*
> *'Our funds are all invested,*

They interest yield each year,
If we should spend our principal
It would end in debt, I fear.'

Then up rose Lady Maxwell,
Softly her accents fell:
'The Charities of Glasgow
Each does its duty well;
But none of them does better,
So sayeth every man,
Than our own beloved Hospital –
The Royal Samaritan.'

'So, build your walls, Directors,
With all the speed you may,
And we will stand on either hand
And help the bill to pay;
We will have a great Bazaar,
Glasgow will do its best,
And we can reckon on much help
From the Counties of the West.

Then men and women, side by side,
Toiled at the mighty task,
Whist drives and concerts, Fancy balls,
Subscriptions too they ask;
And cheques are flying all about,
And many a friend we thank,
And every stall has money made
And lodged it in the bank.

'Look back! Look back!' the Chairman cries;
'Look back!' calls every one,
See the great progress we have made,
Our work is nearly done!
St Andrews's Halls are open wide
The great Bazaar is here,
And even the rankest pessimist
Can scarce forbear to cheer.

While round the stalls buyers crowd,
Holding out eager hands
To grasp some treasured morsel
That on the counter stands.
With shouts of merry laughter
Long shall the tale be told
Of how we raised that mighty sum
In the brave old days of old.

The three-day bazaar again exceeded expectations, raising £78,087. The matrons and the nurses raised £1,400,

Glasgow Police raised £8,462 and other stallholders and new subscriptions accounted for the rest. The surplus was welcome because the revised building estimate for the new wing was £79,000. The capacity of the hospital was now raised to 156 beds. Another expansion in 1936 brought the hospital to its final size with room for 186 beds.

After World War Two, British society began to change in many ways, but for a few years yet, wartime rationing was still in place. In 1947, the hospital directors paid tribute to the ingenuity of the kitchen staff in combating scarcity, but soon the Samaritan began to change with the times.

In the post-war era, husbands and children were allowed to visit together for the first time, a practice frowned upon elsewhere.

In 1948, with the creation of the NHS, the Ladies Auxiliary Association was no longer required to serve the same purpose as before, so they wound up and used their funds to purchase furnishings for the nurses' home. Then they reformed as the Samaritans Auxiliary Association, running both a tea ward for visitors and looking after outpatients.

The Royal Samaritan Hospital for Women was now under the auspices of the Glasgow Maternity and Women's Hospital Board of Management. In the early 1950s, links that had been established decades earlier with general hospitals to provide nurse training came to an end when the General Nursing Council withdrew the Samaritan's status as an affiliated training school. By 1958, trainee nurses would do only the first of three years training at Coplaw Street and return later to do a module in theatre training.

The training may have been reduced but births and surgeries continued at the Samaritan and lab work and diagnostics remained as important as ever.

Back in 1896, when the hospital opened, aspirin had not been invented but in 1956 a new dispensary was required and a full-time pharmacist was employed.

The first full-time physiotherapist was employed in the 1960s.

National Health Service restructuring in 1974 placed the Royal Samaritan Hospital under the management of the Greater Glasgow Health Board.

Catering services evolved as well. In 1974, a plated meal service was introduced which greatly simplified the nurses' work; they previously had to serve all the meals but this created additional work for the catering service. In 1979, a self-service cafeteria replaced the waitress service in the staff canteen.

The Royal Samaritan Hospital for Women closed in 1991, just a few years short of its centenary and then reopened briefly in 1992 as an orthopaedic and general surgery unit for the Victoria Infirmary, but closed again within a few months.

After lying derelict for a few years, the hospital was taken over in 2001 by Govanhill Housing Association. Part of the original section of the hospital from 1895 now serves as the administrative block for the association and its subsidiary Govanhill Community Development Trust, and more recently has also become home to Govanhill Law Centre. Later extensions to the hospital were subsequently converted into housing by the association, some for social rent and some sold to first-time buyers. When those new apartments first became available for purchase, many of which were based in the former nurses' home, dozens of would-be buyers queued overnight in order to be the first in line to bid for new desirable residences overlooking Coplaw Street and Victoria Road.

Pearson's Stores

For many years, Victoria Road was a major shopping centre with a 1912 guidebook describing the thoroughfare as home to *'a cavalcade of emporia'*. For decades, many residents of the area felt no need to journey into the city, because almost everything they needed could be purchased on Victoria Road.

Of the thousands of shops to have traded there over the years, few have made more impression than Pearson's Stores. For nearly 80 years, the family-run business was one of the major retailers on Victoria Road. At the height of their success, Pearson's had five different shops, selling different types of goods, close to each other, with over 7,000 square feet of space, and employing over 100 people. In many ways, Pearson's was the equivalent of a small department store. The first marketing slogan used was *'Everything for the Home!'* and then latterly *'Pearson's Probably Have It!'*

The founder, Tom Pearson, was born around 1888 in Ladybank in Fife and served his apprenticeship as an ironmonger with Hood and Walker in Coupar, near Glenrothes. In 1906, aged 18, he came to Glasgow and worked initially with a wholesale ironmonger called Finnie and Co. before setting up on his own, when he was just 22.

Speaking in the late 1930s, Tom said of his early career:

I had a good training there and my position in business today I owe to the training I got in Coupar. Many interesting and happy days were spent in the county town. Many a bottle of paraffin oil I have pulled on the shop barrow up the Bonnygate and to the South Toll, in the days when oil was more in use than it is today.

My apprenticeship expired in 1906 and I set out to Glasgow to try my hand when I was just 18. After three and a half years' experience in the city, I commenced business on my own, opening an empty shop on the southside of Glasgow. Today we have a very successful store, have developed into china, crystal and furniture departments, have a staff of 41 and last year served 303, 962 customers. Not bad in a short time for a Coupar apprentice.

He opened his first store on the corner of Allison Street and Annette Street with just two other staff. The first Pearson's was an ironmonger and drysalters. A drysalters dealt with chemicals, dyes, soap, salt, preservatives and a wide range of chemicals.

The growing population of Crosshill and Govanhill, coupled with Tom's enthusiasm and knowledge, ensured that the shop was a great success. Tom was far ahead of his time in creating eye-catching window displays and was noted for being one of the first stores in the area to employ a 'stack 'em high, sell them cheap' strategy which proved popular and effective.

His enthusiasm for the business led him to say in an interview with a trade magazine:

Ironmongery is the best and most interesting business to be in. That is why I am in it, and that is why my sons are learning it. The shoemaker declares 'there is nothing like leather'. I say, and say most emphatically, that there is nothing like ironmongery.

New premises were soon required and in 1915 the business moved to a larger store on Victoria Road and soon even that store was not enough. To meet demand and opportunity, they had to extend first on one side then on the other. The store was now selling china and furniture and introduced a gardening section.

As a businessman, Tom was exempt from service during the war, but during his career he held public office and important roles in the business community, including President of the Glasgow and West of Scotland Drysalters Association and President of the Iron, Steel and Ironmongery Benevolent Association. During World War Two he worked closely with the Board of Trade, advising on matters of distribution.

Despite the economic downturn of the 1930s, an additional store was opened next to Crosshill Cinema.

Tom passed away in 1946 and was succeeded as managing director by his son James. James' brothers Tom and David also had management roles in the company.

In the early post-war period, Pearson's continued to thrive adding a paint store and an electrical store. There were now five stores and over 100 employees, all local people, mostly women.

James died in 1962 aged just 47, from injuries sustained during the war. Like his father, he had also been President of the Ironmonger's Benevolent Association but was also a member of the Sporting Car Club and once took part in the Monte Carlo Rally.

Tom and David were consolidators rather than innovators, so rather than expand further the business was reduced a little.

Hardy's took over the furniture store, and the glassware shop was sold but the business continued to be a successful one and even won a number of small business awards.

In the late 1960s and early 1970s new housing was being built in Newton Mearns on the southern outskirts of Glasgow and many Southsiders moved in that direction. This prompted Pearson's to open a store in the new shopping centre at Newton Mearns in 1972. Promoting themselves as Pearson's of Victoria Road, the shop was initially very successful but would close in the early 1980s.

Pearson's continued to be responsive to the needs of the moment. During the three-day week in 1974, when power outages were likely, the store did very well selling stoves and candles. A candle-maker based in the Gorbals was very happy with the business Pearson's gave him at this time.

Tom and David retired in 1981 and James' son, Tom, took over the business. Tom had joined the company in 1961, aged 17, straight from school. Not academically inclined, he approached the rector at Hutchenson's and asked if it was possible to leave at Easter, leading the rector to reply *'What's wrong with now, Pearson?'*. Tom joined the family firm as a trainee in an electrical store, later studying accountancy and taking more responsibility within the company. When Tom was poised to take over, some reconstruction was required; the firm owned 12 flats above the main store and those had to be sold off before Tom could take full control.

The business landscape was changing and competition from other businesses was increasing. Previously, Pearson's had sold lawnmowers but larger firms like Templeton's, now based at Dixon's Blazes Industrial Estate, had greater buying power and could sell cheaper machines, while Pearson's were lucky if they could sell replacement belts for the mowers.

A rival company called M.J. Pearson's from Gallowgate set up business on Calder Street and little could be done to avoid confusion.

Tom brought in computers to make the business more efficient and responsive, joined buying groups to secure better prices and even went to America for a few weeks to study what would become known as 'just-in-time' production. Gradually, the number of suppliers was reduced from over 100 to just 50 or 60.

One innovation Tom introduced at this time was a small restaurant and coffee shop called *Le Jardin*, the first of its type on Victoria Road, which brought people into the stores and helped boost sales. The cutlery section opposite the restaurant was replaced with shelves selling Hallmark greetings cards.

During Pope John Paul the Second's visit to Glasgow in 1982, fishing stools were cleverly sold on as 'Pope stools', so many in the crowd at Bellahouston Park who were there to see the pontiff were able to avoid sitting on the ground.

Tom's wife Moira was a partner in the business and often took charge of creating the window displays in the store. A colleague had told them about Frank Sinatra's final concert in London and how difficult it was to get tickets. Moira had just finished creating a window display for the saucepan company Swan, and to Moira and Tom's amazement won a prize for the display of two VIP tickets for the concert in London, much to the chagrin of their colleague.

During a major refurbishment of the store, the large clock that had hung outside the main store for many years was taken down to be repaired. However, on completion the Council refused permission for the clock to be put up again. That was not the end of Tom's struggles with the Council as rates had been steadily rising and adversely affecting the store's profitability. In 1975, the rates were £7,900, but by 1984 had risen to £56,000 and there were now just 40 staff employed. Tom railed against the increases and tried to keep the business going but on the advice of his accountant, he 'turned the key' in late 1985 and an era was over.

Selling the business as a going concern was not possible, so Pearson's was sold to a construction company who divided the main store up into smaller units.

After the business closed, Tom spent time seeking public office and later moved to Berkshire to work for Kingfisher, a multinational home improvement retail and property development company, whose portfolio includes B&Q and Screwfix.

On retirement, Tom moved back to Scotland and now lives on the Ayrshire coast, playing golf regularly.

Peter the Parrot

Peter the Parrot joined Pearson's in 1952, at the age of two and quickly became a firm favourite with customers, especially children.

Peter, an African Grey parrot, had been recruited to replace two Japanese love birds who had previously been the star attraction in the Pets Department but had sadly died. A red collection box hung on Peter's cage and over his career he raised thousands of pounds for children's charities.

In addition to his charitable work, Peter was a great ambassador for the store. The management believed that today's kids are tomorrow's customers. Many memories of Pearson's Stores begin with fond recollections of Peter the Parrot.

Peter did get in trouble a few times for surprising sensitive souls with some choice language but mostly he is remembered for a cheery 'Hello Boy' or 'Cheerio Boy'.

On one notable occasion, Peter had an encounter with the police force. At night Peter would often be released from his cage to move around the store as he pleased. During one evening, a local police officer was passing in the early hours and noticed the storeroom door was unlocked; peering in he saw a movement in the shadows, and so he cautiously entered the store, expecting to trap an intruder.

The officer crept into the darkened store and was surprised to hear a voice say 'Hello Boy' from the shadows. Believing that he was surrounded by a gang of thieves who had boldly challenged him, he fled to nearby Craigie Street Station and returned soon after with his colleagues to effect an arrest. When the store lights were turned on, Peter was in his accustomed position, inside his cage, and said 'Hello Boy' to the assembled officers.

After the store closed, Peter remained in the care of Tom Pearson, first at Bridge of Weir, then in Berkshire. Peter passed away in 1992.

American Roller Rink

Victoria Road 1908 – 1912

The origins of roller-skating can be traced back to the 18th century as a means to practice ice-skating when there was no ice. Early roller skates were heavy and offered only a limited range of movement. Throughout the 19th century, new designs were introduced such as the three-wheel version, the four-wheel version with axles, or the five-wheel one-line version.

Roller skating went in and out of fashion but the application of ball bearings to a new generation of roller skates by American Levant Richardson in the 1890s allowed greater movement, less friction and more speed. This eventually provided the impetus for the Edwardian roller-skating boom of 1908 – 12, or 'rinking' as it was popularly known.

In those bygone days before permanent cinema buildings, there was a growing interest in everything wheeled; bicycles, cars, aeroplanes and roller skates.

Controversially, 'rinking' demanded looser clothing, challenging the formality of the time. While not exactly a sexual revolution, the relaxing of conventions of the time did allow a little more freedom than before and many people were enticed by the romantic possibilities it offered.

A letter in *The Lady* magazine said:

if a youth possesses good parts, do they not shine to greater advantage in the whirring arena of wheels? If a maiden be graceful doth not her grace become still more charmingly enhanced by the very poetry of motion.

A liberal-minded church minister of the time also praised roller-skating as *'a means of healthy exercise'* and for allowing ladies to exercise their *'latent energies'*. The craze was quickly exploited and 200 companies were in existence by the end of 1908, by 1910, 506 were operating throughout the UK.

Americans Chester Park Crawford and Chester Williams, operating out of Liverpool, set up the American Roller Rink Company. When they were looking to set up a rink in Glasgow, they chose an undeveloped site on Victoria Road, an exciting suburb in the expanding city of Glasgow. They had set up a distinct company for every rink they opened. They formed the Glasgow Roller Skating Company and appointed George M. Wellis as manager, who had been instrumental in bringing the circus Barnum and Bailey's Big Show to Govanhill ten years earlier.

To encourage people into the rink, skilled, 'professional' skaters were engaged to demonstrate and display the art of roller skating, such as Professor H.A. Simmons. The title of Professor was not really an academic distinction but an acknowledgement of his skill and prowess at skating. Simmons was billed as *'King of the Roller Skates'* and gave a display of figure skating and trick skating, including skating on two-feet high stilts and spinning on his toe.

On the evening of December 4th, 1908, skating was postponed for an evening, while a 'Cinderella', a formal ball was staged. The hall was decorated with fairy lamps and flags from many nations, and attendees were issued with 'dainty programmes' which functioned as dance cards.

One journalist reported in early 1909, that:

The Victoria Road Roller Skating Rink continues as a favourite attraction for the youth of both sexes. The pastime is fascinating and exhilarating.

A sport that encouraged freedom, that could be enjoyed by both sexes, led to the blossoming of romance, or at least its possibility.

In February 1909, the manager of the rink, offered *'a special present'* to any couple willing to get married, on skates, in the rink. Whether anyone got married in the rink is at present, unknown.

There was also competitive skating as well as social skating. In February 1909, a one-mile race was held in the rink with cash prizes, and the opportunity to compete in a national competition in London. The race was won by E.K. Rowe, who completed one mile in a time of four minutes and seven seconds.

Rowe was described as:

a lightly-built lad with a neat, nippy style. He took the turns well, and was very fast into his stride on entering the straight.

Glasgow succumbed to the roller skating craze. The rink on Victoria Road was the first in the city, but soon there were several others. Oswald Lindsay, a rink owner from London, visited Glasgow and later said: *'Not to rink (skate) in that city is to be a social outcast'*. Later in the same interview, he also revealed himself as an advocate of temperance, when he said *'rinking is better than drinking'*.

Like many other rinks around the country, the rink on Victoria Road was a metal corrugated shed, so that it was noisy and seasonal, being too hot to use in the summer months.

Nevertheless, the business directory *Glasgow 1909* ran the following advertisement:

One of the most popular resorts in Glasgow today is the American Roller Rink conveniently situated in Victoria Road with a car stopping place at the main entrance. Although only a few months in existence it is already in the favourite haunt of thousands of the best people in the city. It owes its inception to Messrs C.P. Crawford and F.A. Wilkins who have promoted several similar enterprises throughout the country with conspicuous success. The skating surface which measures 300 feet in length by 100 feet wide is constructed of fine maple, specially imported from Maine USA which gives a remarkably smooth top. Several hundred pairs of the famous Samuel Winslow Ball Bearing skates are maintained in excellent order for the use of patrons at the pastime is indulged in with great enthusiasm by the old and young of both sexes. The popularity of the rink may be gauged from the fact that the first fancy dress carnival was attended by 700 skaters and 3000 spectators.

No doubt part of the success of Glasgow enterprise is due to the amiability and discretion of Mr George M. Wellis the resident manager. As might easily be imagined an undertaking of this sort could easily be spoiled by loose management but of that there can be no such danger as long as Mr Wellis is in command. His experience is as interesting as it is extensive, he having been connected with some of the largest amusement enterprises in America such as Barnum and Bailey's Big Show etc. He keeps watchful eye on all kinds of undesirables with the result that the best people in this city go to the rink with absolute confidence. Roller skating is delightfully pleasant recreation and that imparts grace and health is admitted by all who have attained even a slight proficiency in the art. Fine music is supplied by a military band both afternoon and evening.

The admissions policy may have been questionable; the *'undesirables'* were probably the many Irish who were arriving in Glasgow at this time and inevitably there was much debate about the morality of skating.

The magazine *Rinking and Rinks* said in an editorial in 1911:

The rinking situation is a delicate one. The killjoys and spoilsports are abroad in the land. It behoves resident managers and rink proprietors to proceed cautiously lest they fall. Allied with the puritans will be those hurt by competition with the rinks. Rinking will have enemies. We wish roller skating to continue as we believe it at present to be a clean, healthy sport, a clean, healthy business.

In 1911, the Victoria Road rink was the scene of a scandal that rocked polite Glasgow society and absorbed the chattering classes for weeks. A young Glasgow heiress, daughter of a prosperous soft-furnishings merchant and justice of the peace, who was *'exceedingly well known in* local society circles' became acquainted with a young instructor at the rink. Despite living in the west end of the city, she was seen skating, almost on a daily basis at the rink on Victoria Road, in the company of the handsome, young instructor. Fearing her father's disapproval, the couple eloped to Edinburgh where they were married and then journeyed on to London, at first living in a hotel in West Kensington. Their romantic bliss was short-lived; if they had chosen a less conspicuous location, her father and his solicitor may not have tracked them down so quickly. Despite having means of her own, the young woman returned to her parental home.

Rinking remained popular for another year or so but inevitably, like every popular craze, public interest began to wane. The recession, a failure to develop a summertime use for the building and, most significantly, the advent of permanent cinemas, were significant factors in the impending closure. The Majestic had just opened a few streets away.

For the directors of the Glasgow Roller Skating Company, it was time to diversify. On Whitsunday 1912 they leased the building to J.J. Bennell, the cinema entrepreneur for £375 per annum for two years, £400 thereafter and by September, the BB Cinerama, Govanhill's second and largest cinema opened for business.

Cinema City

From 1897 to 1910 new entrepreneurs, emboldened by new moving picture technology such as the animatograph, travelled from city to city, from town to town, from hall to hall, bringing the new spectacle of film to the nation.

At first, there was little in the way of stories being told in these early films. Often the travellers had a camera and filmed local people in the street in the afternoon, then invited them to come to their local hall in the evening to see themselves on screen. Dixon Halls was noted as hosting such a film show in 1911.

The first purpose-built cinema in Glasgow was the Charing Cross Electric Theatre on Sauchiehall Street, which opened in 1910. By 1939, there were 114 picture houses in Glasgow with seating for 175,000, more than any other city in the world. Glaswegians went to the cinema on average 51 times a year. Scots in general went only 35 times a year, and across the UK the average was only 21 times a year.

For most Glaswegians, there were two cinemas within walking distance of their home. Rival cinemas would often try to attract people away from their competitors' queues. Cinema was popular across the classes. For many working-class families, the warmth, comfort and recreational space they provided was cheaper than staying at home with the lights on all night.

Cinema going declined in Glasgow from the 1950s onwards as greater wealth for some people at least meant more recreational options.

Houses were of a higher standard and television was becoming increasingly common. Hollywood itself was changing, the Westerns, so popular with Glasgow audiences, had been replaced with darker more pessimistic fare such as film noir and melodrama.

Majestic Theatre

**110 Smith Street
(now Inglefield Street)
Architect: A.V. Gardner (1912)**

Arthur Vivian was a cinema owner and entrepreneur. In 1910, he formed the Scottish Moving Pictures Company and in 1912 opened two cinemas; one in Rosyth Naval base, and in July of that year The Majestic in Govanhill.

The manager of the Majestic, Mr T. Robertson, wrote the following preview of the opening of the cinema in the industry magazine *The Bioscope*:

> Vivian's Picture's is one of the most enterprising cinematograph concerns in Scotland – just as Mr Arthur Vivian, its managing director is one of the most enterprising individuals in the same line. The Majestic at Govanhill, Glasgow is the latest venture of the company mentioned to be opened.
>
> Internally, The Majestic leaves nothing to be desired in the way of comfort and Govanhillites should not admit to make the new Vivian hall one of their weekly calling places. Luxurious tip-up chairs supplied by Messrs. Whiting and Bosisto of Bristol, have been fitted up throughout the auditorium and every patron has a clear an uninterrupted view of the screen.

The first film that was shown at The Majestic was called *Saved by Fire*, a drama about a young oil prospector, battling against a giant corporation, trying to make his small piece of land profitable. Mr Robertson, the manager went on to write of the film *'this splendidly ingenious piece of cinematography aroused, as was to be expected, the keenest and liveliest enthusiasm and admiration'.*

Patrons who could afford the one penny entrance fee would come in the front door, but for the less affluent entry could be secured by offering two half-pound 'jeely jaurs' (jam jars) or one single-pound jar. If someone paid this way, they would have to come in the side entrance and sit on a wooden bench near the front.

By 1914, Arthur Vivian had moved onto new challenges, leaving Robertson in charge and the cinema prospered for several more years. There were twice-nightly shows often showing short films produced by the Famous Players / Lasky Corporation or variety hall acts on film. However, in the face of competition from larger and more well-equipped cinemas the Majestic began to struggle and was sold in 1933.

Through a lack of attention or investment, the reputation of The Majestic began to decline. When it was sold to a new owner in 1940, it was described as being *'badly worn and smelling of urine'* which may explain why it was nicknamed 'The Styx'. If the experience of entering The Majestic was like crossing the River Styx, which unfortunate souls had to cross to reach the underworld, then it must have been a dank, dark place indeed.

The Majestic closed as a cinema in 1957 and was used briefly as a dance and bingo hall before being used as a temporary location for mass. Closing finally in 1969, work started on preparing the site for a new church, however a fire brought that task to a swift conclusion, or perhaps it was a divine retribution. Until very recently, it was used by the Our Lady of Consolation parish. Now there is new housing where The Majestic once stood.

existing building was converted, a building that had been in place since the 1890s.

The interior was refurbished to become a cinema and a new grand façade put on the front to tempt cinema-goers.

Before 1920, before it became a cinema, it was the premises of Duncan & Youill, a ladies' and children's outfitters. Back in 1894, W. C. McKenna, a clothier and outfitter traded from that address. This original purpose may go some way to explaining why there were a number of windows down the side of the building, overlooking the railway platform, windows that have long since been bricked up, windows that surely had little or no purpose in a cinema.

The elegant façade concealed a ridiculously long interior with a cramped balcony. This unusual shape required the projector to be placed at the rear of the auditorium, which was apparently an advantage with images being less affected by the thick smog which still afflicted the city, especially on still winter days before The Clean Air Act of 1956. However, the awkward shape of the building, lack of facilities, and the noise of trains passing, did little to help Crosshill Picture House succeed and it closed in 1952.

In an unforgivable but perhaps inevitable act of vandalism, most of the façade was removed and the building was converted for retail use. Initially it became a furniture store and in later years, in a nod to its cinematic origins, it was a branch of the Blockbusters video store, and at the time of writing it is a successful hardware store.

An inscription acknowledging the architect Joseph Boyd, can still be seen on the side of the building from the stairs down to the train station.

Crosshill Picture House

488 Victoria Road
Architect: Joseph Boyd (1920)

Crosshill Picture House, perched above Queen's Park train station was opened in 1920 by J.M. Drummond who also owned The Crown Cinema in Gorbals.

In those early days of cinema, each new venue, each new picture palace that opened had to look enticing, like a theatre or a Spanish hacienda or an Egyptian temple, the outside had to hint at the exotic adventures available within. The Crosshill Picture House had a classical exterior, like a theatre or opera house but this wasn't a brand-new establishment on a previously unoccupied site, an

Hampden Picture House

91 Westmoreland Street
Architect: John Eadie (1920)

Plans for the Hampden Picture House were announced in February 1920, and £25,000 of shares were issued at £1 each.

There was some negative reaction in the press at the time, that yet another cinema was to be built. The *'mad craze of kinema'* was condemned as *'neither educative nor morally uplifting'* and that *'the picture house is the curse of the age'*.

The Hampden opened on the 3rd of January 1921 was designed *'on a scale to rival other houses in Glasgow'*. The 'bug resistant, leather tip-up seats' seats were supplied by J.H. Robinson from Possil Road.

The manager, Mr William C. Tetley, worked hard to ensure unique programming at the Hampden. In the foreword of one of the early weekly programmes, Tetley wrote:

> If a man can write a better book, preach a better sermon, or make a better mousetrap than his neighbour, though he built his house in the woods, the world will make a beaten path to his door.

He went on to describe the Hampden as *'the premier suburban picture house in Glasgow'* and as a venue *'where the sun of originality never sets'*. There were two shows a night from 6.30pm and matinees on Tuesday and Saturday at 3.00pm. Newsreels were supplied by a company called Topical Budget.

The curtains covering the screen were still opened by turning a hand crank when the cinema closed in 1969. The exterior was plain but one or two fine details could be seen in the signage such as the Roman numeral V instead of U.

Like many other cinemas, The Hampden was repurposed and became a bingo hall, then later an Irish social club called The Clada, and finally a dance and social hall, the Up-and-Down Club. The cinema was demolished in 2007 and the empty site became a small park, now known as Westmoreland Park.

BB Cinerama (LL)
New Cinerama
Odeon Eglinton Toll

201 Victoria Road/Butterbiggins Road

Architects: Alexander McInnes Gardner/ J. Campbell Reid (1922), James Lindsay Ross (1931 enlargement with new entrance)

Expectations were high for the new BB Cinerama, finally, after a prolonged planning and building period, the doors opened on the 7th of August 1922.

With seating for 1,800 people, it was for a while at least, the largest cinema in the country. A few days later, *The Bioscope* proclaimed it *'Glasgow's Best Yet'* and went on to report:

> The new Cinerama is the best word in picture houses in Glasgow. In size, in appearance, and in simple beautiful decoration it will rival anything in the Kingdom, while for the convenience of patrons nothing has been omitted.
>
> From the back of the auditorium to the screen is 130 feet while the width of the hall is 100 feet, the widest public building in the city.
>
> The huge balcony is supported on immense girders, strong enough to carry a railway train, and has no pillars supporting it to obstruct the view of patrons.
>
> Projection is from the back to a seamless screen and perfect pictures were obtained. The main entrance is a marvel of spaciousness and it is questionable if there is a bigger entrance to any cinema theatre in existence. The colour scheme in the picture house proper is white, cream and gold, the panels being most artistic.
>
> On each side of the screen organ lofts, which will be occupied by a powerful instrument in due course, but which meantime makes a very decorative feature of this end of the hall.
>
> Mr Frank Wolstenhulme who managed the old Cinerama so well, will have charge of the new house and while he is naturally proud of the handsome building, he parted from the old house with regret.
>
> The contractors for the various works of special interest to cinema folks were; electric rubber flooring etc, Ioko Rubber Company, Glasgow, painting, Henderson & Son, Pollokshields, seating FBO Ltd and Robinson, Glasgow area and Paterson, Glasgow Ltd (balcony)

J.J. Bennell died in December 1922. In his obituary published in the magazine *Scottish Kinema Record* it was said of him:

> In making Scotland his home he did our country proud, for, whether by Association with our countrymen or natural attributes, he had many of the characteristics typical of a Scotsman. He was shrewd, he revelled in hard work, possessing an honesty of purpose in all that he did that could not help having an influence on those with whom he came into contact.

Despite the loss of their founder, the cinema remained a great success.

Mrs Morag Blakeman recalls attending in the 1920s:

I went with my mother on Friday afternoons. The film was usually a serial. The Count of Monte Cristo was my favourite and I wouldn't have missed it for anything. The circle seats cost ninepence and free tea and biscuits were served in the interval. They were passed along the aisles by the usherettes and people in the know sat close to the end of the rows to get most of the biscuits.

The BB was sold to Gaumont in 1929, who redesigned the building for the talkies and increased capacity to 2,062. In 1931, they also created another entrance on Victoria Road.

In 1948, J. Arthur Rank's Circuits Management Association took over and changed the name to New Cinerama. In 1964 it was remodelled again, removing many original features and reopened as Odeon Eglinton Toll. The capacity was also reduced to 2,003.

By the 1970s, only the balcony was used, and with attendances down to as little as 12 a day, it closed with a screening of *Snow White and the Seven Dwarves* in October 1981. Rank wanted to convert the building to a music venue, but despite the closure of the Apollo in Renfield Street, Glasgow District Council vetoed the plans and it was demolished in 1986. The site was converted to a petrol station for a period. Work to redevelop the site in 2007 briefly revealed remains of the winged globe which once adorned the entrance. In 2018, new housing was built on the site.

Calder Cinema

302 Calder Street
Architect: Cowiesons Ltd (1932)

The Calder opened on 25th April 1932 and stood back-to-back with the Govanhill Picture House. Along with several other cinemas in Glasgow, the new cinema was built in a Spanish Colonial style, capped by a red-tiled roof, with seating for 1,250.

The first owner and promoter of the Calder Picture House was James Hamilton, owner of a small chain of cinemas which included Ardgowan Picture House in Weir Street, Tradeston. He also owned the Govanhill Picture House, which may go some way to explaining why another cinema was permitted to be built so close to an existing one, virtually back-to-back with the house on Bankhall

Street, Hamilton almost certainly already owned the land but by the time the Calder opened, Hamilton had sold his interest in the Govanhill Picture House.

Shares were issued in February 1931 and £6,000 was raised for the new cinema, making it one of the least expensive cinemas to be built in the area and it was complete in just three months.

There was seating for 1,223 people, 640 in the auditorium and 583 on the balcony. Other cinemas in the area certainly had expensive conversions to make, when sound was introduced to movies in 1929, but the Calder would have been built with the new equipment required in mind. Sound was provided by Western Electric and there were two Kali projectors and Roxy reproducers.

There was no formal opening ceremony but shortly afterwards an article appeared in the *Kinematograph Weekly* which described the look of the building in great detail, without acknowledging or recognising that it was clearly designed to look like a Spanish hacienda.

The most interesting point made in the article, concerning the facade is that *'the name appears in red on a background of polished black'*. In the interior it was noted that:

...the proscenium opening is boarded with a narrow band of black and gold with a ray design and colour above the screen.

The first manager was Mrs Diamond, who was transferred from the Ardgowan Picture House, where she had been responsible for all the bookings on the Hamilton circuit. Her tenure was a brief one and she was succeeded shortly afterwards by Mr Archibald Fleming.

The Calder often showed second-run releases, or serials such as Tom Mix or Flash Gordon that ensured the loyal custom of a younger audience.

In 1933, the cinema was taken over by another promoter, Harry Wincour, who at the time, lived on Nithsdale Road.

A year or two later, the new owner was in trouble with the Inland Revenue for allegedly filing false tax returns. However, in his obituary in 1951, he is still noted as a cinema proprietor. He died in Cannes, leaving property in England, Scotland and abroad, and a fortune of over £250,000.

The Calder was sold to Green's, a rival chain, shortly after Wincour's death and then became a bingo hall in 1967, finally closing in 1972. Looking worse for wear, it was demolished in 1981.

Continued on page 75

1. Water colour of Govan Iron Works, sometimes known as Dixon's Blazes, by
William Simpson, painted in the late 1840s.

2. The coat-of-arms of the Burgh of Govanhill, which
existed between 1877 and 1891.

SKETCH MAP

OF THE CITY OF GLASGOW

AND ITS ENVIRONS.

1885

NOTE.—The Area within the Parliamentary Boundaries is coloured .... LIGHT RED.

The Areas of the Municipality which lie beyond the Parliamentary Boundaries are coloured DEEP RED.

The Areas beyond the Municipality which are subject to Glasgow Police Jurisdiction are coloured, so far as within the County of Renfrew, ... BLUE.

So far as within the County of Lanark and Police Burgh of Govan, ... BLUE.

Suggested Parliamentary Boundary

187 ST. VINCENT STREET.

GLASGOW, FEBY. 1885.

3. A map of Glasgow and the surrounding burghs in 1885,
prepared for the Boundary Commissions Inquiry.

QUIZ SUPPLEMENT, 16th MAY 1890

DR. MARWICK'S "TIDDLEDY-WINKS:" THE LOST GAME.

4. Sir John Marwick, Glasgow's Town clerk, playing tiddley-winks, trying to work out
how to bring the burghs that surrounded Glasgow, under the city's control.

5. Govan Iron Works, sometimes known as Dixon's Blazes in the 1950s.

6. Postcard showing workers leaving the North British Locomotive Company
factory, commonly known as the Dübs factory.

7. A newly completed locomotive, an 0-4-0 built by Dübs & Co. at Glasgow
Locomotive Works, part of an order for two from China (1886).

8. A locomotive under construction, a 3' 6" gauge 4-8-2 built by the North British Locomotive Co. at Queen's Park
Works, part of an order for 60 placed by South African Railways (1945).

9. Photographic print of a street scene: a new locomotive, a 4-8-0 for the Benguela Railway, secured on a special cradle as it leaves Queen's Park Works at the start of the journey to Glasgow Docks (1930).

10. SS Chauncy Maples at anchor on Lake Nyasa (1905).

11. This shows the frontage of the Sentinel Works from the south-west. The five-storeyed block was built as a pattern shop and store, and offices, and was designed by Archibald Leitch. It was the first reinforced concrete building in Glasgow. To the right are machine and erecting shops (1970).

12. Larkfield Omnibus Depot (1931).

13. Govanhill Baths on Calder Street (1917).

14. The opening ceremony at Govanhill Baths on 28th February 1917,
featured a display of swimming by Mary Strathearn and Bella Muir,
holder of all Scottish records at the time.

15. The main pool or 'Big Pond' as it was known at Govanhill Baths (c.1920s).

16. A baptism at Govanhill Baths, led by Pastor Gilbert T. Fletcher (1928).

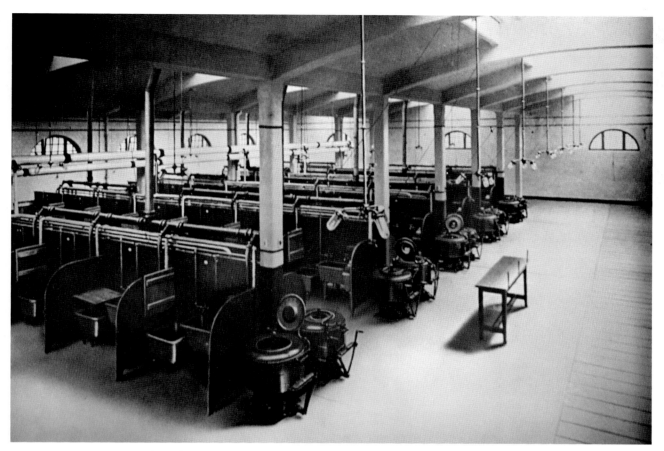

17. The steamie at Govanhill. A view of the washing stalls (1917).

18. The steamie at Govanhill. A view of the drying-racks (1917).

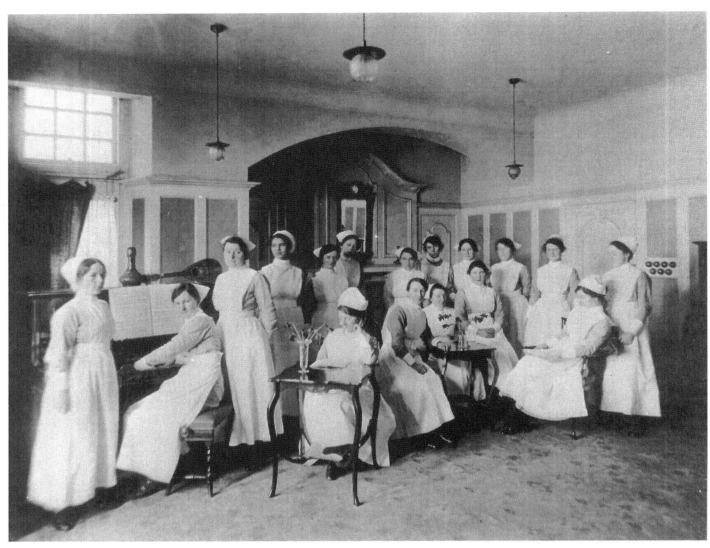

19. Nurses at the Royal Samaritan Hospital for Women (1917).

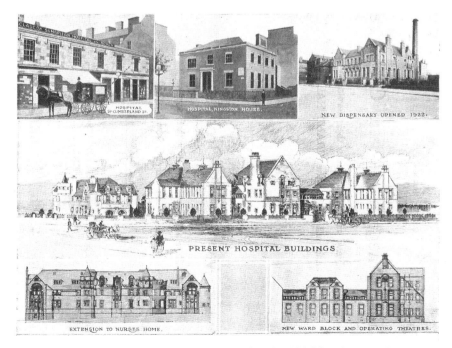

20. Illustrations from the programme for the 1924 fundraising bazaar,
showing the first and second hospital, the existing hospital prior to extension
and the proposed extensions.

21. Staff at Pearson's main store on Victoria Road in 1959, marking the 50th anniversary of Pearson's Stores, just above the sign, the edge of the large clock that hung outside the store is visible.

22. 'Everything for the Home' – Pearson's advertising slogan on the side of a tram, (c.1959).

23. Pearson's main store on Victoria Road (1984).

24. Peter the Parrot (1984).

25. The American Roller Skating Rink on Victoria Road, taken from the Cuthbertson Street junction (1909).

" If you would be Graceful, learn to Skate."

American Roller Skating Rink,

Victoria Road (South-Side), Glasgow.

HIGH-CLASS ROLLER SKATING.

THREE SESSIONS DAILY.—10.30 a.m. to 12.30 p.m. ; 2 to 5, and
7 to 10. Military Band, Private Garage. Afternoon Teas.
Free Instructions. Five Books containing 60 Tickets for Admission
or Skates, £2.

26. Advert for the American Roller Skating Rink on Victoria Road (1909).

27. Staff at the American Roller Skating Rink on Victoria Road (1909).

28. Aerial view of The Majestic (c.1960).

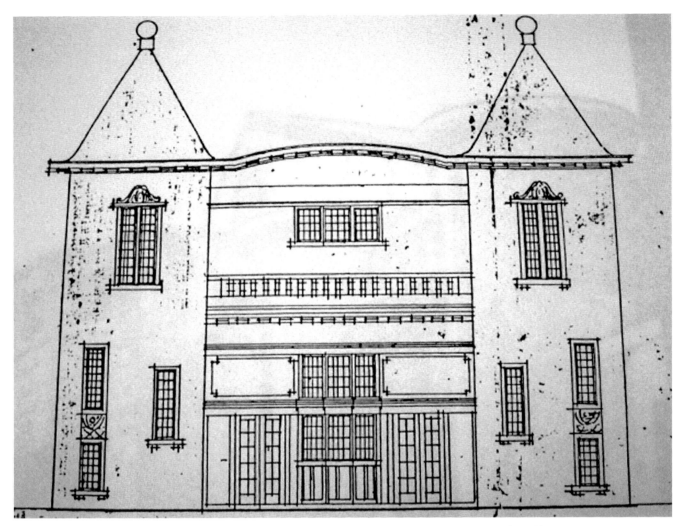

29. Design for The Majestic on Smith Street, now Inglefield Street (1912).

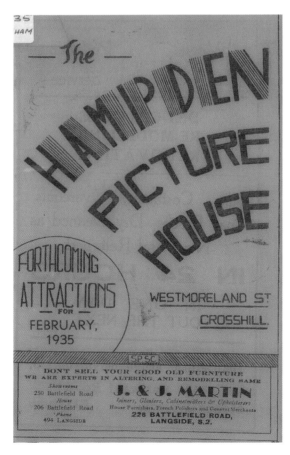

30. Cover of Hampden Picture House programme for February 1935.

31. Crosshill Cinema (c.1920s).

32. The Calder Cinema on Calder Street (1980).

33. The former Hampden Picture House on Westmoreland Street, pictured in the 1980s when it had been converted to the Clada Social Club.

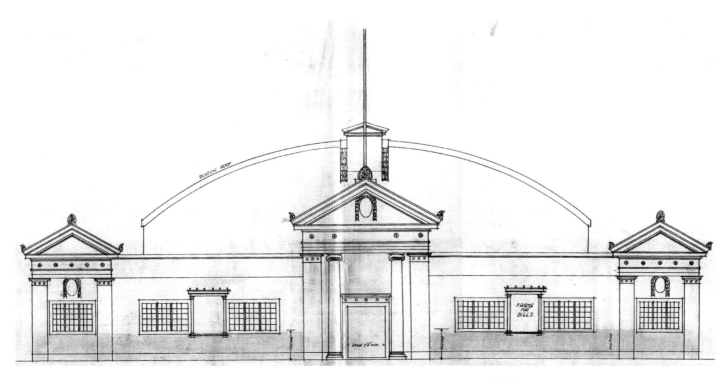

34. Architectural design for the first BB Cinerama (1912).

The Govanhill, Glasgow.

35. The Govanhill Picture House on Bankhall Street (c.1926).

Victoria Road showing B. B. Cinerama.

36. The BB Cinerama on Victoria Road (c. 1912).

37. The second BB Cinerama on Victoria Road at the junction with Butterbiggins Road (c.1922).

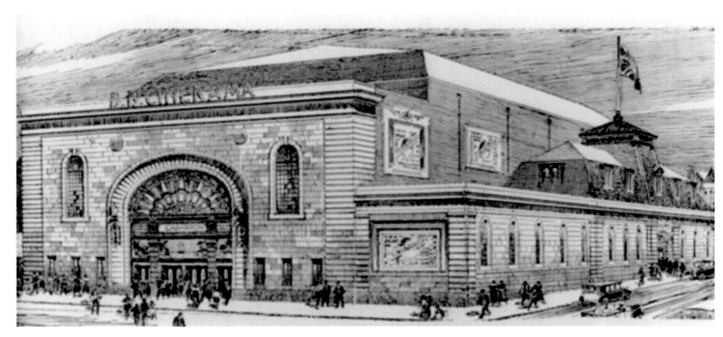

38. The BB Cinerama on Victoria after the 1931 extension.

39. Scotland vs. England at Old Cathkin Park, in the Illustrated Sporting and Dramatic News (1884).

40. Scotland vs. England at Old Cathkin Park (1884).

41. Celtic vs. Rangers in the Glasgow Merchant's Cup Final in 1895 at Cathkin Park.
The spire of Dixon Halls can be seen in the background, above the tenements.

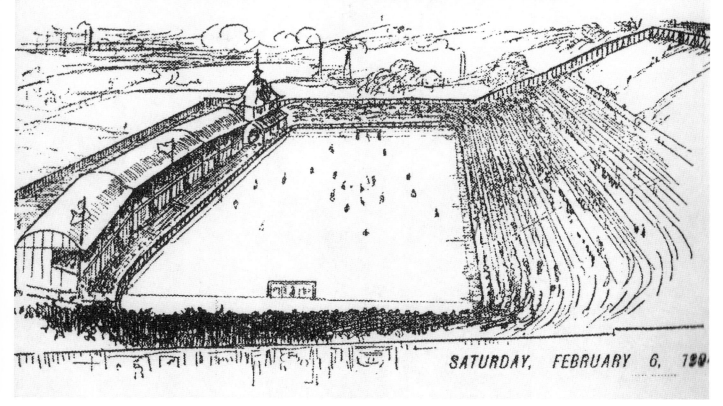

NEW CATHKIN FOOTBALL PARK.

A SPLENDID GROUND—COMMODIOUS AND SAFE.

SATURDAY, FEBRUARY 6, 190

42. Drawing of New Cathkin Park.

THE VICTORIA BATH CLUB
GLASGOW
T. L. Watson architect Glasgow

43. Victoria Baths on Butterbiggins Road (1881).

44. Interior of Victoria Baths (1906).

Fig. 39.

A. Turnhalle.
B. Hof.
C. Waſchküche.
D. Mangelraum.
E. Abort.
F. Wäſche-Magazin.
G. Aſchenlager.
H. Kohlengelaſs.
I. Sudatorium.
K. Keſſelhaus.
L. Tepidarium.
M. Shampooing-Raum.
N. Waſchraum.
O. Brauſe.
P. Treppe zur Sprungbrücke.
Q. Sprungbrücke.
R. Wannenbäder.
S. Frigidarium.
T. Aborte.
U. Schwimmbecken.
V. Waſch-Cabinet.
W. Aborte.
X. Auskleideraum für Herren.
Y. Haupteingang.
Z. Eingangshalle.
AA. Verwaltungs Bureau.
BB. Raum zum Abſtellen der
Schuhe.
CC. Sprechzimmer.
DD. Wirthſchaftsküche.
EE. Auskleideraum für Damen
und Kinder.
FF. Flurgang.

Victoria bath zu Glasgow[110].
Arch.: Walſon.

45. Diagram of the interior of Victoria Baths.

46. Interior of The Plaza, with the fountain in the centre of the dance floor (c.1923).

47. William Wilson, the first Baths Master at Victoria Baths (c.1877).

DANCE AT

The "PLAZA"
Palais De Danse
EGLINTON TOLL, GLASGOW.

Every Afternoon, 2-30 to 5 p.m.
Admission, 1/6 (except Saturday Afternoon, 2/-).
Dainty Teas Served at City Prices.

Monday, Tuesday and Thursday Evenings.............Dress Optional......2/6
Wednesday (Novelty Night)—
Dress Optional......3/6
Friday Evening——Evening Dress......5/-
Saturday Evening...Dress Optional......5/-
Dancing from 7.30 p.m.
Two Famous London Bands.
"The Cuban Moons." "Reso's 'Frisco Five."
Dancing Partners. Luxurious Tea Lounges
Book your Tickets and Tables NOW at "PLAZA" Box Office. 10-12 noon daily, or Telephone Queen's Park 1000.

LEARN TO DANCE
A large staff of Expert Lady and Gentlemen Instructors available daily, 10 a.m. till 12 noon, to teach quickly all the newest Dances.
TERMS VERY REASONABLE.
Arrange Your Lessons at Once.

48. An advert for newly opened Plaza Ballroom (December 1922).

49. Alex Freer, resident bandleader at the Plaza from the late 1920s to the late 1930s.

50. Crosshill and Govanhill Burgh Hall (1879).

51. Dixon Halls (1896).

52. Belleisle Street Station, on the left, now a boxing club and Belleisle House
on the right (2019).

53. Queen's Park 'G' Division at Craigie Street Station (c.1897).

54. Firemen at Queen's Park Fire Station (1944).

55. Queen's Park United Presbyterian Church (1878).

56. The interior of the Queen's Park United Presbyterian Church on Langside
Road, a collaboration between Alexander Thomson and the celebrated
Victorian decorator, Daniel Cottier.

57. A drawing of Crosshill Synagogue from the cover of the brochure celebrating the laying of the foundation stone in 1960.

58. The interior of Crosshill Synagogue in 1963, with the ceiling mural painted by Alasdair Gray.

THE NEW WORLD—ITS FOUNDATIONS TO BE

LOVE TO BE THE SPIRIT OF ITS INHABITANTS

The Young Socialist

A MAGAZINE OF JUSTICE & LOVE

Vol. IX.—No. 5.   Glasgow, May, 1909.   Price One Penny

59. The banner of the Young Socialist magazine, the official newspaper of the Socialist Sunday School movement.

60 The Govanhill Socialist Sunday School during the
May Day parade (1936).

61. Design for the Air Force Auxiliary Headquarters at 49 Coplaw Street (1925).

62. The Avrom Greenbaum Players production of 'Chicago' at Coplaw Street (1984).

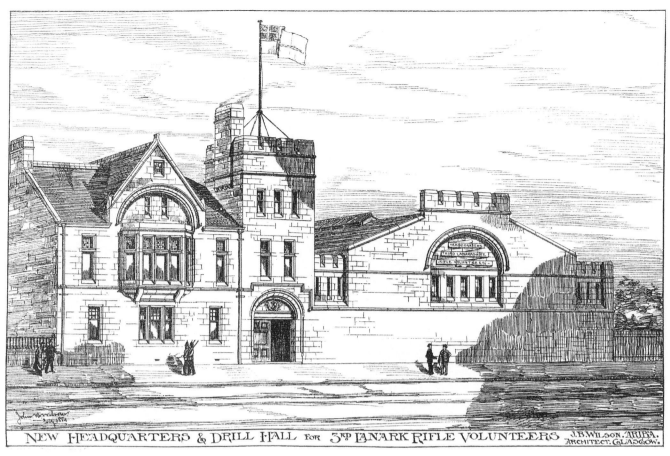

63. The Headquarters and Drill Hall for the 3rd Lanarkshire Rifle Volunteers (1884).

64. 'M Company' of the Third Lanarkshire Rifle Volunteers, outside the Drill Hall on Coplaw Street (1904).

65. The Headquarters and Drill Hall for the 1st Lanarkshire Volunteer Artillery on Butterbiggins Road (2019).

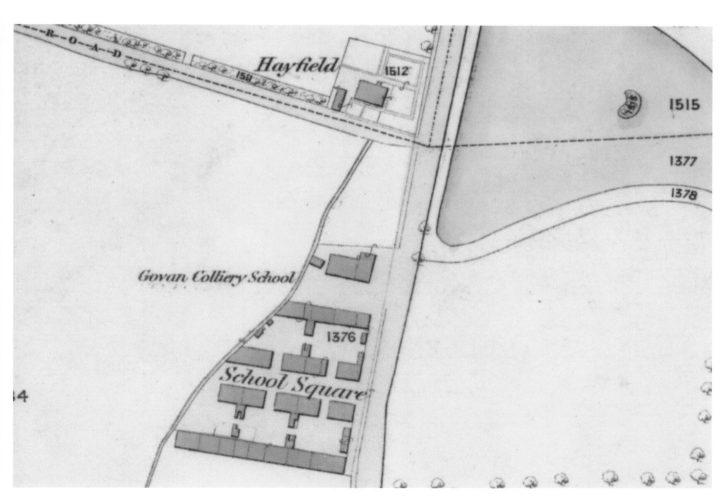

66. Map of Cathcart Road from 1858, showing the Govan Colliery School, just south of the junction with Butterbiggins Road.

67. The original Calder Street School, built in 1874, the oldest surviving building in Govanhill.

68. Crosshill House, photographed around 1920. The original part of the house was
built in 1739 but several extensions were built in the 19th century.

69. Promotional material for Charles Mitchell's photographic studio, the Queen's Park studio on Victoria Road. The Tudor-style building is now a betting shop, next to the train station.

70. A photograph of two girls taken at Charles Mitchell's Queen's Park Studio, c. 1899.

71. The bandstand at Govanhill Park, c.1913.

72. Govanhill and Crosshill District Library, which opened in 1906.

73. The boy's reading room at the Govanhill and Crosshill District Library.

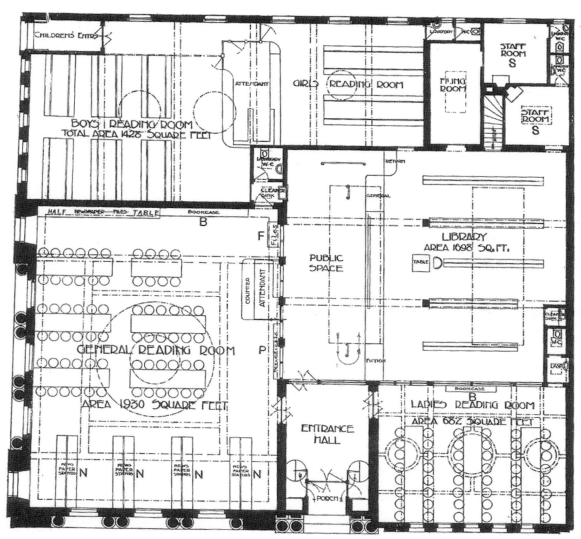

74. The original layout of the Govanhill and Crosshill District Library.

75. On the left, the original Holy Cross chapel school on Daisy Street, built in 1883. The larger building on the right, is the second chapel school, which opened in 1900. Both buildings are now part of Daisy Street Neighbourhood Centre.

76. Holy Cross Church on Dixon Avenue, which opened in 1911.

77. This building on Langside Road, at the corner of Queen Mary Avenue was once known as the Marie Stuart Hall, which opened in 1876.

78. A steam train arriving at Queen's Park Station (1955).

79. The signal-box at Queen's Park Station (1960).

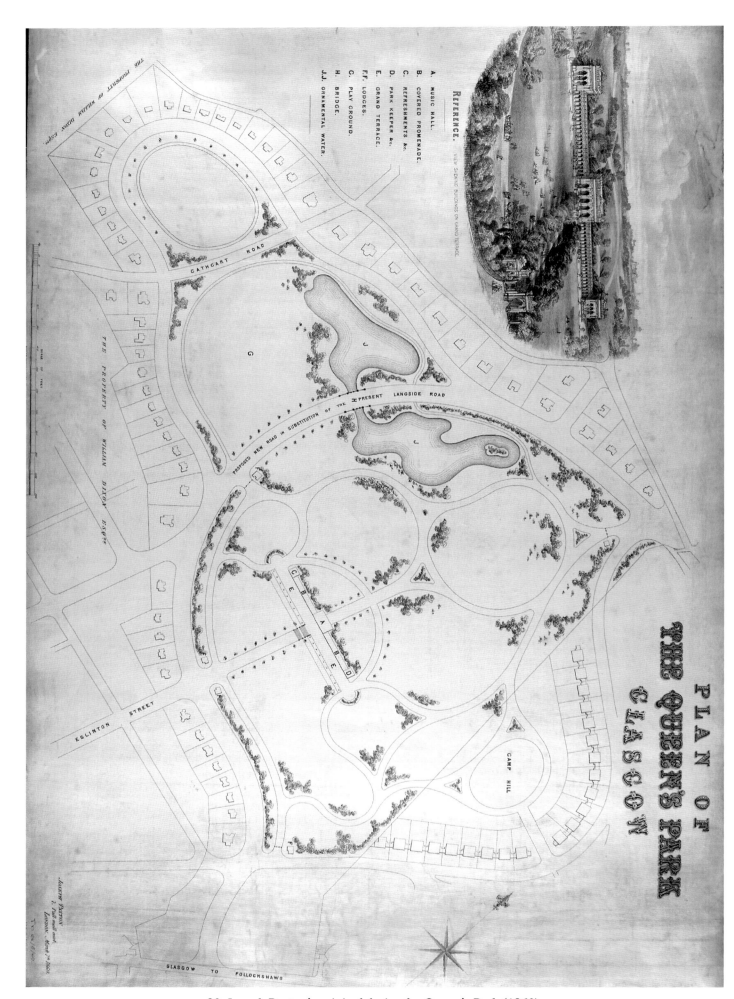

80. Joseph Paxton's original design for Queen's Park (1860).

81. Detail from Paxton's original design for Queen's Park (1860).

82. The view from the top of the steps in Queen's Park, looking north to Victoria Road and Glasgow, circa 1876. Taken by renowned Victorian photographer, George Washington Wilson.

PROPOSED CONSERVATORY IN THE QUEEN'S PARK, GLASGOW

83. Detail of the interior of the Kibble Palace, which was originally intended for Queen's Park, circa 1871.

84. The second bandstand in Queen's Park, circa 1913.

85. The gates at the Victoria Road entrance to Queen's Park, c. 1936.

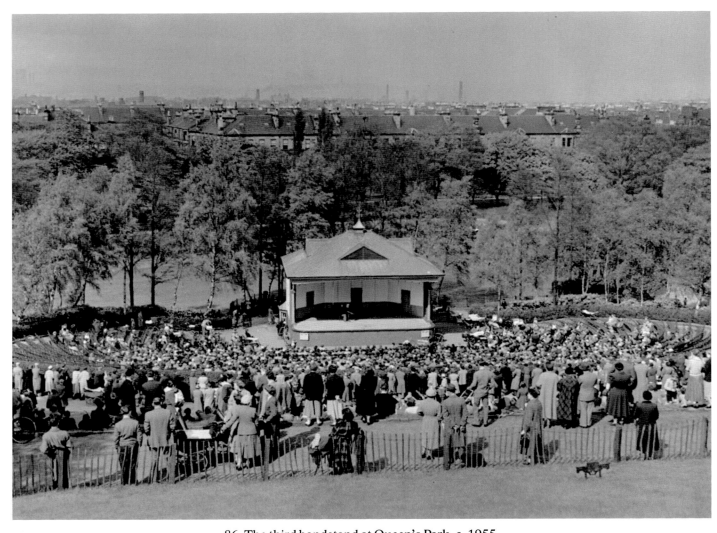

86. The third bandstand at Queen's Park, c. 1955.

87. A family enjoying the sunshine at Queen's Park, date unknown.

Govanhill Picture House ABC

49 Bankhall Street
Architect: Eric A Sutherland (1926)

The fourth cinema in Govanhill was the Govanhill Picture House, which opened its doors on the 2nd of May 1926. It was a project initiated by the Govanhill Cinema Company Ltd and was led by James Hamilton who already owned the Ardgowan Picture House in Tradeston, Govan Cross Picture House and the Camphill Picture House and would later go on to open the Calder Picture House.

Hamilton and the board needed to raise £25,000. The building would cost £15,000, (nearly a million pounds in today's money) and the ground would cost £8,000, (equivalent to nearly half a million) so shares were sold in their new venture; 24,950 preferred shares were available at £1 each and 1,000 ordinary shares at one shilling each.

One reason they were given planning permission even though the area was well served for cinemas was the growing popularity of cinema, this was still long before television and Govanhill was much more heavily populated than it is now – there was upwards of 40,000 people living locally and even more new houses were about to be built so they felt success was assured.

Their projections were very optimistic, of 1,213 proposed seats they predicted selling 737 seats at nine pence each on Saturdays the cost would rise to one shilling. Then they would sell the remaining 476 seats at six pence each, their predicted profits were going to be £6,552, or about £400,000 per year. It didn't quite work out that way, by 1927, the company had gone into liquidation and was eventually bought over by the ABC chain who had contracts with Warner Brothers and MGM.

The Dean of Guild who gave approval to build the cinema said 'it will be completed in a comfortable and artistic manner'. The architect was Eric Sutherland and he let his imagination run riot.

In those days cinemas had to be enticing and attractive. Tutankhamen's tomb had been discovered four years earlier and there was still a craze for all things Egyptian. The Govanhill was the first cinema in Britain to be constructed in an Egyptian style.

It was also one of the first cinemas where the stalls and the balcony ran together, there was not that separation, except where it came to price.

On the 20th of May 1961, a film called *A Song Without End*, a biographical drama about the composer Franz Liszt and starring Dirk Bogarde, was the last film shown at Govanhill Picture House. Then perhaps inevitably, it became a bingo hall, until 1974. Then it lay derelict for a few years before it became a retail outlet but it is still one of the most striking buildings in Govanhill. Most of the interior has been demolished but the façade is listed and a few, small original spaces remain.

BB Cinerama (1)

Victoria Road/Cuthbertson Street
Architect: J. Campbell Reid (1912)

When the American Roller Rink closed in 1912 it was taken over by J.J. Bennell, who had been a manager of travelling cinema shows since the early 1900s. It was basically a large corrugated shed with a neo-classical façade.

Only about two-thirds of the original rink was converted to use as a cinema but the change of use was handled well and the *Glasgow Herald* praised its conversion:

> ...a pretty decorated vestibule with tea rooms on either side gives access to the auditorium. Also very effectively designed, seating accommodation is provided for about 1500 people and in respect of heating and ventilation everything has been done for the comfort of visitors.

There were also 42 private boxes and room for 100 people standing in the promenades.

The BB Cinerama was the first recognised cinema brand in Scotland. The initials B.B. stood for Bright and Beautiful and Cinerama had nothing to do with the later widescreen process of the same name. Ticket prices in 1921 were between sixpence and one shilling.

J.J. Bennell was more than a cinema owner, he was an inveterate showman and was called 'the father of the trade' amongst Glasgow cinema owners. In those days of silent films, he would create special sound effects behind the screen and would also read out dialogue to enhance the drama of the film being shown.

The first manager of the Cinerama was a popular figure called Mr. Frank Wolstenhulme, who was always to be in the foyer, greeting the audience, when the cinema opened. The cinema and the programming attracted many favourable reviews.

In May 1914, the *Bioscope* reported:

On Wednesday evening I looked up Mr Wolstenhulme at BB Cinerama Victoria Road, and found him in charge of what is one of the most charming and convenient halls it has yet been my lot to visit.

Items on a programme which was attracting full houses were; the 'Vicar of Wakefield', 'Outwitted by Billy', 'The Girl and the Houseboat', 'Construction of an Engine', 'The Girl and the Tiger', 'Fatty's Affair of London', 'The Upward Way and 'A Vivaphone Singing Picture'.

Verily the Cinerama fulfils its description on the programme – 'A lordly pleasure house wherein at ease you are entertained'. I shall look forward with pleasure to my next visit to the Cinerama'.

When the First World War was declared, Wolstenhulme was among the many who volunteered to serve, even though he was close to the upper-age limit.

In his absence, the *Bioscope* reported:

The cheery presence of Mr Frank Wolstenhulme is much missed, but Frank has a bigger job in hand at present and the King's uniform has taken the place of the dress suit. Mr. J.J. Bennell and Mr. Lawton however, carry on between them with Mr. Temby as substitute manager and supervisor of staff.

In December 1915, screenings were postponed for an evening while the Cinerama hosted what was described as the '*social event of the year*', at least in the cinema trade. The reason for this event was the eighth anniversary of the opening of another of Bennell's cinemas – the Wellington.

The evening's entertainment included a supper, a whist drive and dance, with a variety programme in between. A variety artist and comedian called Wallie Frame was the headline and apparently he kept the audience '*in a state of hilarity*'.

Speaking in 1917, Bennell said:

I opened, five years ago, a house in Victoria Road, large and airy, and comfortably equipped, and have had no reason to complain of lack of patronage. I had pinned my faith to the working classes and the twice nightly house, and I did not dream that the palatial picture house, as we know it today, drawing its tens of thousands of patrons, would ever become a reality. I was entirely wrong.

Bennell pioneered Saturday matinees, which attracted great audiences to afternoon shows. The children's screening began with singing the BB Pictures Song:

BB Pictures, they're all right,
Come and see them every night
We will sing with all our might
BB Pictures they're all right!

Frank Wolstenhulme was demobbed in February 1919 and returned to his duties on Victoria Road. The Saturday matinees were the forerunners of the later cinema clubs that hosted many children's talent shows over the years, particularly at BB Cineramas around the country. Bennell also introduced a dividend scheme for children to gain loyalty points or free gifts. On Christmas Days he was known to give a medallion souvenir and even free boots and socks to needy children.

The Cinerama was a hugely popular venue, but its days were numbered; the large metal building was only ever intended to be a temporary structure, and crucially the land on which it stood, which was owned by Glasgow Corporation had been earmarked several years earlier for new housing. The population of Govanhill was growing rapidly and new houses were urgently required.

This was far from the end of Bennell's cinematic enterprise on Victoria Road, in fact, it was just the start of a new chapter. He acquired the lease of another plot of the Corporation's land, just 150 yards further north on Victoria Road at the junction with Butterbiggins Road, on the condition that he build '*a first-class cinema*'. Bennell readily agreed, new luxurious cinemas were opening around Glasgow and he was keen to compete, but the planning process was lengthy and he faced a series of obstacles and objections before final approval was granted.

Identifying when the original Cinerama finally closed for business has been difficult but it was known to be still operational in the summer of 1921, and was in all probability still showing films in early 1922, right up until the new Cinerama opened in April of that year. Some houses in the Coplawhill area were probably built around the cinema before it was finally demolished.

Old Cathkin Park

The first international football match was played between Scotland and England in 1872, on a cricket pitch in the west end of Glasgow. This match inspired thousands of people across the city to form clubs and take up football. Soon Glasgow was described as *'a city full of errand boys forming clubs with grand names and playing games on coups and vacant railway arches'*.

Football quickly became 'the people's game'; it was easier to play than cricket, which had been popular, and did not need pristine pitches or facilities for a game to start. It was rough and exciting, the perfect game for the working classes of Glasgow.

The Third Lanarkshire Rifle Volunteers were one of the clubs formed in the wave of enthusiasm generated by that first international match and they had an advantage over many other clubs as they had a drill ground where they could play football. Records show that the club's first ground was called Victoria Park; this may have been part of their grounds in the Coplawhill area, with an entrance on Victoria Road. Maps of the period only show an area of land belonging to the regiment, surrounded by a brickfield. Cuthbertson Street and Kingarth Street, along with the schools on those streets, were not built until the early 20th century, so it is perhaps impossible to know exactly how the area was used in 1872, or to be certain of the precise location of Victoria Park.

What is certain is that by 1873 the club was using another ground, just off Dixon Road (probably called Bankhall Park at the time), part of which they turned into a football pitch; present day Boyd Street now runs through the middle of where that pitch used to be. Just a few years previously, this ground was part of the Govan Colliery site belonging to William Smith Dixon but was now being used largely for housing. Dixon rented space to the club to use as a drill ground and football pitch. It is possible the pitch was used by the brigade and by another club that sprang up around this time, Govanhill Lacrosse, later known as Govanhill FC, whose ground is listed as Bankhall Park.

By 1878, the rifle volunteers were the team with a growing support. With the help of William Lorimer, the owner of Queen's Park Locomotive Works, a grandstand was constructed, then a pavilion, open seating and an embankment were built to form a stadium that would become known as Cathkin Park. It was, at this time, one of the best stadiums in Glasgow.

There was even an early experiment in floodlighting at Cathkin. According to reports, at an evening match against Vale of Leven in November 1878, just three weeks after the very first floodlit match at Bramall Lane in Sheffield. Something called the Gramme system was used to illuminate the action at Cathkin. In all probability, this was a large searchlight owned by the regiment. The experiment was partially successful but one light on its own was not sufficient and it was many years before lights became

standard at Third Lanark matches or any other Scottish football ground.

The first Cathkin Park was chosen for many important matches during its short existence. In season 1881 – 82, it was the venue for the Scottish Cup Final (and the replay) when 14,000 people saw Queen's Park beat Dumbarton by four goals to one. In 1884, it hosted two British Home Championship matches, the first on 15th March, when Scotland beat England by one goal to nil. This was the 13th international between the two countries and the *Scottish Athletic Journal* proclaimed that the match *'has surrounding it more interest than any of its predecessors'*. The report goes on:

> The crowd began to pour out to Cathkin Park at a very early hour. I myself arrived a minute or two before the teams and on my way out in a hansom, seeing very few people with their faces towards Crosshill, I naturally assumed the game was about to be a failure from some unknown cause or other. This impression was quickly dispelled when I entered the open gate. The sight that met my eyes convinced me that the enthusiasm of Scotland is as great as ever when the prospect of seeing a first-class game arises. The three stands, reserved and otherwise, were all filled when I put in an appearance only to be followed onto the field by the contestants of the day.

No photographs exist of the match, but a photo of the two teams was taken, either before or after the match and an artist called John Swain, illustrated episodes of the match for the London Illustrated News. There are glimpses of the uncovered stands, of journalists with bowler hats, of the Burgh Hall in the background, and of carrier pigeons taking results and reports quickly into the city.

Two weeks later on 29th March, Scotland beat Wales by four goals to one. The report states:

> The ninth international between Scotland and Wales has ended like its predecessors in a victory for Scotland. Somehow Wales had never been able to make anything like a stand against the representatives of the Thistle, though occasionally she comes off best in her encounters with England. Of course, all local matters gave place to the great event and consequently, the followers of the dribbling game were to be found at Cathkin Park. In far greater numbers than the importance of the match warrants the result being looked upon as a foregone conclusion. About five thousand people witnessed the match, about half the number that assisted at the

English International.

In 1885, Third Lanark Rifle Volunteers achieved their highest ever victory in a game against St. Andrews, winning by 11 goals to nil. When the Scottish Football League was formed in 1890, Third Lanark were one of the founder members, the fifth club to join the league.

In the very first league match at Cathkin Park, the home team welcomed Dumbarton – one of the best teams in the country – as opponents, but they lost the game by three goals to one. Third Lanark finished fifth in the league that season but Cathkin Park hosted a play-off to decide the title between Dumbarton and Rangers who had finished equal on points. That match finished in a draw, two goals each with the teams being jointly awarded the championship.

Very few photos exist of Cathkin Park, but the clearest one taken is from a game played in 1895, the Glasgow Merchant's Cup Final between Celtic and Rangers, which Celtic won by four goals to nil. In the background of the photo, the spire of Dixon Halls can be seen over the rooftops, while a small cottage, where tenements now stand, reveals part of Cathcart Road.

Around this time, the football club, looking to turn professional, cut ties with the regiment and renamed themselves Third Lanark Athletic Club.

While the club may have owned the stadium it did not own the land on which it stood. New housing was urgently required in the area, and so Third Lanark were given notice to quit Cathkin Park by the end of the 1902 – 03 season. An article in the magazine *Scottish Referee* in August 1902, reported that:

Third Lanark's directorate have been prospecting during the past few weeks for new ground. They have had a long occupancy of their present Cathkin camp, having been occupants there since 1873, their field before that being situated in Victoria Road, to the north of Allison Street where at one time, the Third Lanark Rifle Volunteers actually held a camp during the summer months. Owing to the rapid growth of dwellings in Govanhill, ground is extremely difficult to procure but we hope that Third's Directorate will be successful in securing new quarters.

Their near neighbours and keen rivals Queen's Park Football Club had been refused permission to develop their ground at Hampden Park and had bought a new plot in Mount Florida, so the obvious solution to Third's predicament was to buy the stadium being vacated by Queen's Park.

Over the 1902 – 03 season, a tense situation developed between the two clubs; Queen's Park's asking price for their old stadium was £1,000 but Third Lanark were only prepared to offer the considerably lower amount of £350. In consequence, at the end of the season Queen's Park auctioned off their stadium and all the fixtures, they had hoped to sell the stadium as a complete unit for £1,000, but were obliged to sell it in parts raising only £400.

Third's final league game at Cathkin Park was played on 4th April 1903 against Dundee but this dispute over prices left the ground that Third Lanark hoped to occupy, completely empty.

A journalist from the *Glasgow Observer* reported:

The Queen's old ground has been stripped of every shed of furnishing and the playing pitch now lies open to the four winds of heaven. I'm afraid the Third Lanark will regret their hesitation to give £1000 for old Hampden as it stood.

Third Lanark had no option except to build a new stadium. They could have walked into a ready-made stadium for £1,000 but the new stadium including what they could salvage from Cathkin Park would end up costing over £3,000.

Unfortunately, they had been required to quit Cathkin Park at the start of the 1903 – 04 season and so arranged to play their home games at Kilmarnock and other venues, until their new stadium was complete.

Queen's Park also unexpectedly found themselves homeless because the opening of the new Hampden Park had been delayed. Some of the tension that existed earlier between the two clubs over pricing was dissipated when special dispensation was agreed, to allow Queen's Park to play their opening home games at Cathkin Park which had not yet been demolished.

Queen's played their opening games of the season at Cathkin Park. The final match played at Cathkin was in October of that year, between Queen's Park and Partick Thistle, the match ending with both teams scoring one goal each.

Queen's Park then moved to Hampden Park and returned the favour they owed to Third Lanark by sharing their new ground with them for the next few months, allowing their rivals to play matches at Hampden and train there for two days a week.

In the meantime, the original Cathkin Park was finally demolished, many fixtures and fittings were saved and used at the new stadium, including the main grandstand which was transported, mostly intact, the short distance down Cathcart Road, by a large team of horses.

The new stadium would become known as New Cathkin Park, was rebuilt in a slightly different position, 30 yards further south of where Queen's old stadium had stood. The capacity of New Cathkin Park was 50,000.

The club had hoped to attract a high-profile club such as Newcastle to play the opening game at the new stadium but Scottish Cup commitments meant that Third's first game at New Cathkin Park took place on 6th February 1904 when they played Alloa Athletic in the third round of the Scottish Cup.

With the passage of time, the new ground became known simply as Cathkin Park and the first stadium, in Govanhill, would be remembered as Old Cathkin Park.

Victoria Baths

The first swimming pool in Govanhill was the privately-owned Victoria Baths on Butterbiggins Road. The building was designed in what was called an Oriental Moorish style by architect Thomas Lennox Watson.

Watson notably went on to build the Citizen building on St Vincent Street, one of the first buildings in Glasgow constructed from red sandstone. He is also credited with designing part of the City Chambers.

What little is known about Victoria Baths, shows just how different Govanhill was in the 1870s, an attractive suburb of Glasgow. The middle-class residents of Crosshill, near Queen's Park, fleeing the smoke and squalor of the city, would have welcomed this little bit of luxury to the south side.

The Victoria Baths Company was formed on the 20th of October, 1875, principally by south side based members of the Arlington Club, a private swimming club in the west end of Glasgow, who wanted a swimming club closer to where they lived. The new company set about the work of raising money and finding a suitable plot of ground. The proposed capital required was £10,000 and 2,000 shares were offered for sale at £5 each.

At a public auction in 1876, they acquired the site on Butterbiggins Road. Construction began in 1876 and in an early report it was claimed:

> ...the new building will have a fine, two-storeyed frontage to Butterbiggins Road and will present an elegant, external appearance. Care has been taken in the arrangement to express the dual character of the erection – the bath and the club – and something of an Oriental air has been imparted to every divi-

sion of the work.

The final cost of construction was £11,125, furnishings cost a further £800.

Victoria Baths opened informally in the summer of 1877 and was described as occupying *'a commanding site with a breezy background of far-stretching fields'*.

Indoors, the pond hall was 100 feet long and 140 feet wide. The main swimming pond measured 75 feet long by 36 feet broad, and was six feet deep at one end and three feet deep at the shallow end and was surrounded by 33 dressing boxes. On the east side of the building were hot and cold baths which were under floor level, with steps to descend into them, rather than *'clay, iron or enamelled contrivances'*. The Turkish suite, which would contain the latest means of heating and ventilation, was not yet complete. Upstairs contained a reading room, smoking room, billiard room and galleries on both sides of the main pond.

The formal opening took place on Saturday the 2nd of February 1878, when the Turkish Baths were complete. Two days later the *Glasgow Herald* reported:

> The Victoria baths on Victoria Road were formally opened on Saturday afternoon. For some time members have had the use of the swimming pond, the hot baths and the gymnasium but the Turkish baths have only now been completed and various details which remained to be carried out when the baths were partially opened have since been executed. The gathering on Saturday therefore was of the nature of an inauguration of the new buildings. On the invitation of the directors a large number of ladies and gentlemen were present. The large swimming hall was decorated with tree ferns and other plants kindly lent for the occasion by Mr A.B. Stewart of Langside and seats placed around the pond for the accommodation of ladies.
>
> The galleries overlooking the pond were also crowded with spectators. Ex- Baillie William Wilson discharged the duties of chairman and amongst other gentlemen present were the honourable W. Collins, Lord Provost (who however required to go away before the proceedings were far advanced), Provost Brown of Crosshill, Provost Wilson of Govan, Dr A.L. Kelly, Mr Hosie of Mauldside and Mr A.B. Stewart. The chairman made a few remarks and declaring the baths completed and open to subscribers. He congratulated the directors on the success of their labours and remarked that the baths for their size were as complete as any of the kind in

the Kingdom, if indeed they might not be said to be the most complete. (Applause)

The number of bathers who had taken advantage of the baths since the opening of the establishment on the 15th of September last was 13,292 or an average of 2984 per month. Arrangements were in progress whereby the baths would be reserved one day each week for ladies. (Applause)

The Lord Provost next spoke, alluding in complimentary terms to the part which ex-Bailie Wilson had taken in connection with providing baths for the great mass of the people and expressing the hope that the last undertaking in which he had been engaged, that of Victoria Baths would prove successful. Mr William Wilson, club master, and his brother afterwards went through an interesting series of performances in the water. The brothers Wilson are remarkably clever swimmers and their illustrations on Saturday of diving, fancy swimming, swift swimming and how to rescue a drowning person were highly appreciated by the large assemblage. The method of using the trapeze was also shown by two gentlemen members, one of whom, failing to seize a flying trapeze, flopped down into the swimming pond, from which he presently emerged, dripping and laughing.

The company then inspected the building, all parts of which were thrown open for this purpose. We have already described the baths in detail and may only now mention that on the ground floor of the swimming pond are hot baths, Turkish baths, slipper baths and club masters rooms, while on the upper floor of the reading room, billiard room and smoking room period. All are handsomely furnished, the Turkish baths look especially eliciting favourable comment. There is no extravagance anywhere. Every room is marked by quiet elegance and maximum of comfort.

William Wilson, formerly baths master of the Arlington Baths in the west end of Glasgow, was appointed master of the new building when work began in 1876.

Wilson was a tireless campaigner for the right to swim and the health-related benefits of swimming. In his book *Swimming, Diving and How to Save Life*, the first comprehensive swimming manual, published in 1876, he says:

Of a truth, swimming should form part of the education of every boy and girl, not only as a healthy and lively accomplishment, but also from motives of prudence and safety. Why should the women of this country not enjoy the privilege of indulging in such an exercise, and thus be in the possession of that which would enable them more practically, to understand the first law of nature, self-preservation and know how to save their own lives in cases of accidental immersion?

Notably, Wilson also codified the rules of aquatic football, or what would later become known as water polo. There was a game of water polo at the opening ceremony of Victoria Baths in 1877.

Wilson died in 1912 but Victoria Baths continued to operate until at least the outbreak of World War Two. A newspaper article from 1940 reports the trustees had decided to close the building for the duration of the conflict because so many members were now involved in the war effort or on active service.

It is unknown if but highly unlikely that the baths reopened after the war, but by this point in time there would have been one of the biggest cinemas in Glasgow on one side, a church on the other and one of Glasgow's largest bus depots, the Larkfield Depot just across the road, and in addition, many, many new tenements and shops would have been built in the surrounding streets. The public baths at Calder Street, which had opened in 1917, would also have provided some competition and a viable alternative for many. A busy, bustling city was rebuilding and reinventing itself after the war. The idyllic retreat outside the city and the *'far-stretching fields'* of 1877 was long gone.

Victoria Baths was finally demolished in 1952. Subsequently, there was a tennis court on the site where the baths had been and that was in place at least until sometime in the late 1960s. The site is now, at least partially occupied by an ambulance station.

The Plaza
'Palais de Dance'

The Plaza opened on 27th December 1922, not the first dance hall in Glasgow but the first grand 'palais de dance' with a lavish interior, multi-coloured lighting system and a steel sprung floor.

There would come to be 11 dance palaces in Glasgow over the next decade, including Green's Playhouse, Barrowland Ballroom and the Locarno. Louis Freeman, a prominent bandleader who supplied small orchestras for picture houses and ships, made his money at the smaller Berkeley Ballroom in Glasgow and used his profits to open the Plaza.

There were two resident bands brought in from London, *The Cuban Moons* and Reso's Frisco Five.

The first major event at the new venue was the New Year Ball on 1st January 1923. You could get *'dainty teas at city prices'* and you could book a lesson with a professional dancer. At some halls a lesson would cost just sixpence but at the Plaza a course of lessons would cost one guinea (£1 and one shilling) for a course or five shillings for each one.

In the afternoon session, between 2.30pm and 5.00pm, there were 26 dances, equating to one every six minutes. You could tell the time by looking at the number of the dance.

The dancers-for-hire were not professionals in today's sense of the term, but were recruited solely on their dancing ability. They earned £1 per day, plus a cut of the fee for every dance, and also earned gratuities from grateful customers, such as shirts, shoes and dresses. In the early 1920s income tax was just sixpence in the pound, so it was a fairly lucrative occupation.

Sometime in the late 1920s Alec Freer became the resident bandleader at the Plaza. Alex Freer and his band's performances were regularly broadcast on national radio, on the National Channel. They made recordings for the record label Decca and they often toured the country to great acclaim, but the Plaza was their homebase until 1939.

The 1920s was still a very formal time, a working-class man would come home from work and press his dancing trousers before tea, then put Brylcreem in his hair and part it down the middle.

At major dance competitions, dress was always formal but the Plaza always insisted on evening dress. Chiffon cost a shilling a yard, with some dresses using as much as 30 yards, while the cost of a design was typically about five guineas.

In the 1930s, styles began to change. New dances such as the Lindy Hop and the Jitterbug became popular, representing a departure from the formality of ballroom dancing.

In 1931, the Rhumba was performed at the Plaza for the first time and was described in the *Glasgow Herald* as *'an erotic dance with violent, sinuous movements of hip, shoulder and torso'*. Rhumba classes soon became very popular.

The Plaza famously boasted a fountain in the middle of the dance floor and dancers quickly learned not to stray too close or they would get wet.

Bands visiting and working in other ballrooms around Glasgow would frequently have an early evening performance in the city and then come along to the Plaza for a late-night show. The renowned band leader Joe Loss and his Orchestra made an annual visit to the Plaza for nearly 50 years.

The outbreak of war in 1939 put a stop to all entertainments in the city for a few weeks but then people cautiously ventured out again and the venues reopened.

Initially, matinees and tea dances in the afternoon were more popular and evening sessions were shorter. Boys picked up their dates from home and carried a handy torch in their pocket in the event of a blackout.

The Plaza also broke a long-standing tradition and allowed less formal dress on Friday evenings, but this practice was soon discontinued and a slightly modified rule was reimposed and dancers had to wear either evening dress or uniform.

As the war intensified, Glasgow began to enjoy its biggest dance boom in years and the Plaza enjoyed capacity attendances throughout the conflict, doubtless aided by opening late, till 1.00am every evening, it was the only dance hall in Glasgow to open so late during the war, as long as transport permitted.

American troops brought new dances, new energy and not a few fights to the dance halls of Glasgow, but the formality of dress and style at the Plaza remained. The Grand Charity Ball in 1942 raised £1,800 to support Prime Minister Churchill's Aid to Russia Fund.

In 1952, new manager Adam Sharp, recently arrived in Glasgow from Aberdeen, had the innovative idea of starting a formation dance team called Starlight Formation. This dance team always performed to music that referenced stars or the sky, such as *When You Wish Upon a Star* or *Dancing in the Dark*. Their specially choreographed routine would include the ballroom lights being suddenly dimmed and to the amazement of the audience, the ladies' dresses would light up.

Despite the advent of Rock 'n' Roll, ballroom dancing remained popular in the 1950s and beyond, thanks to television shows like the Television Dancing Club and later Come Dancing, but from the 1970s onwards, evening sessions were given over more and more to concerts and discos, with formal dancing limited to afternoon sessions.

Pink Floyd played at the Plaza in 1971, other bands to have graced the stage include the Fall, New Order, Gary Numan, Suede, Manic Street Preachers, Blur, Supergrass, Shed 7, Kula Shaker and many more.

A former doorman recalled working one night in the 1980s when he heard a loud bang. He turned to investigate and saw a figure falling from above and landing in a cloud of dust in the middle of the dance floor. It was a young man who had been stripping lead from the roof, fortunately still alive. When asked where he came from, he simply said *'Up there!'*

In 1992, Scottish and Newcastle Breweries acquired the Plaza, by now the last of the great halls where ballroom dancing could still be enjoyed. The ballroom dancing continued in the afternoons, as well as gigs, discos and raves in the evening, but by the mid-nineties the Plaza looked dilapidated, a poor shadow of its former self. It closed before the decade was complete.

The building lay derelict until 2006 when demolition began, in order to make way for 76 new houses. The developers promised to retain many original features but, in the end, the whole interior was demolished and only the façade of the building was retained and subsumed into a larger design. The new flats opened in 2007 and the design has been widely condemned. Architectural magazine Prospect voted the new Plaza as the worst new building of 2009.

Crosshill and Govanhill Burgh Hall

One of the most distinctive local buildings in the area is what is now called Dixon Halls on the corner of Dixon Avenue and Cathcart Road. Built in 1879 and designed to serve the new burghs of Crosshill and Govanhill, the hall was the gift of William Smith Dixon, proprietor of Govan Iron Works and owner of most of the land in the area. The purpose of the new building was principally to serve as a space for the transaction of the municipal business of the two adjacent towns, which, because of their growing populations, had recently achieved burgh status. It also provided a social space for residents of the district. Designed in a Scots Baronial style by architect Frank Stirrat, the hall cost £20,000 to build and was opened on 12th December 1879 with a grand ceremony. The building had no official name at first, the press referring to it as the new Crosshill and Govanhill Burgh Hall, but it was only on 24th December 1879 that the board of trustees decided to adopt the name Dixon Halls.

It was Dixon's wish that the two communities he had nurtured, who did not always see eye-to-eye with each other, would have a place to meet and discuss their differences and to socialise and grow closer.

The new legal status of the burghs also required them to have the means to deal with what Dixon called *'the unruly element in any populous place'*, so the precise location of the hall was very important, because lawbreakers had to be tried in the area where they had committed their crime or misdemeanour. So, the new hall intersected the boundary of Crosshill and Govanhill, of Lanarkshire and Renfrewshire, with separate courthouses in each burgh, though both under one roof. Around the same time, the first police and fire station in the area was built at the rear of the Burgh Hall, on Belleisle Street.

At the opening ceremony, attended by over 400 people, the title deeds to the building were handed over to the officials of the two burghs. William Dixon was not in attendance but his deputy read the following letter:

Gentlemen, – it is with great regret that I am obliged to place these few remarks in the hands of a deputy and that I cannot have the pleasure, on account of the present state of my health, of meeting you all this evening. The object of my inviting you here is that I may place in your hands as Commissioners for the Burghs of Crosshill and Govanhill the title deeds for these courts and hall. I need scarcely mention to those present that deep interest that I have all my life taken in this part of my property – the place in which I spent all the early years of my life, and which I have seen changed from green fields to two extensive and populous burghs. Nor need I bring to your memory the many fights I have had with you in defending our independent existence. Now that these burghs are decided institutions, I have felt that there was one great want to be filled up in the shape of proper meeting rooms, where the inhabitants could discuss their interests and have their social gatherings without being dependent on their large city neighbour. Besides this, there is always a certain unruly element in all populous places, however well behaved, which require the administration of the law, and which necessitates having courts of justice. It then struck me that a properly constructed building containing these requirements would be necessary for these districts; however, a difficulty then presented itself, namely, that the burghs were in different counties, and, according to law, justice must be dispensed in the county in which the crime is committed. To avoid as far as possible, the building of two sets of public offices, I determined to find out a site so that each courthouse could be in its own county and at the same time have all the other buildings under one roof. This caused rather a large area of building than would have been required for a single courthouse, and before placing the roof upon it I determined to introduce a large hall, where all might have their social gatherings and entertainments. This hall I trust you will 'warm' this evening. Now, having given you a few words on what I may call the rise and progress of the buildings, I have little more to do than to beg that you, as representatives of the inhabitants of these burghs, will accept them from me, and that they may long continue to be of service to the people. I now hand you the title deeds, and, in conclusion, trust that you may all have a very happy evening, and that many such evenings may be spent under this roof. I have also to thank you for the honour you have done me in accepting my invitation.

I remain, faithfully yours, W. Smith Dixon.

In reply, Provost Browne of Crosshill thanked their benefactor and spoke proudly of the idea of local government as a means of empowering a community and how he hoped the occasion would inspire a sense of local patriotism. On the partnership with Govanhill, he hoped *'an indissoluble band'* would be formed and that the two burghs, now wedded together through the gift of the halls, would *'maintain towards each other that kindly feeling which is the unfailing characteristic of a united and happy family'*.

Provost Smith of Govanhill reiterated Provost Browne's thanks to Dixon and then admitted he was one of the oldest residents of Govanhill. He claimed when he first came to live in the district, just 13 years previously, in 1866, he found *'three self-contained houses, a few miner's houses and green fields'* but in 1869 a transformation began and just ten years later Govanhill's population had swelled to 10,000. He concluded by saying:

tonight we stand forth as the goodly burgh of Govanhill, free and independent but resolved to hold out the olive branch of peace and to live in harmony with everyone around.

The evening concluded with a concert by the Crosshill Musical Association – and there may even have been some dancing.

There was certainly dancing in the years that followed, much of the social life of the area centred on the Burgh Hall, at least it did for certain classes of society.

Each year, the upper hall was the venue for the Conversazione of Govanhill West Ward (a dinner dance really). A joint ticket for a man and a woman cost seven shillings and sixpence; ladies could get an individual ticket for two shillings and sixpence. Tea would be served at 7.30pm, dancing would begin at 8.00pm, and carriages would arrive at 2.30am to conduct guests home.

For those less inclined to dance, an extensive menu one year included a fish course: dressed cod and oyster sauce or filleted soles. This was followed by mutton cutlets and tomatoes or curried chicken then a choice of roast beef, corned beef, turkey and tongue or chicken. For the sweet, there was plum pudding, hot apple souffle, Swiss tart, German tart and then jellies or cream fruit to finish.

Apart from the grand Conversazione, the minute book of the board of trustees reveals a little of how the hall was used in those early years.

One of the first issues to be dealt with was the appointment of a hall-keeper who would live on-site. William Dixon had recommended Sergeant McLaren, orderly room clerk of the 2nd Lanarkshire Militia who was about to retire from the service. The trustees met with the sergeant and initial discussions seemed to go well so he was invited to apply for the job. Though McLaren's references were acceptable, for some reason that is not recorded, the references for his wife, who would also live on site, were not, so it was then decided to advertise the job, with an annual salary of £65. Applications received numbered 510, with 21 people short-listed, though it is not recorded who eventually got the job.

Some applicants to use the hall are recorded in the minute book, such as Govanhill Choral Society, Crosshill Good Templar and Temperance Society (a group promoting abstinence from alcohol), a drawing class and even Queen's Park Football Club, who used the hall for a number of years as the venue for their annual ball. The *Scottish Athletic Journal* reported on the ball in 1884 and said that:

The Burgh Hall is not the perfect ballroom imaginable but it is the best in the district. The Hall on Wednesday last presented quite a brilliant spectacle. The company was select, the ladies costumes pleasing, nearly all in good taste and many of them rich while the fine plant decorations, supplied by Messrs McDonald and Sinclair of the Crossmyloof Nursery, gave an added brightness to the scene. One of the best features of the ball was its representative character. Representatives were present from most of our leading clubs. Nothing will so augment the good feeling that already exists between the Queen's Park and other important clubs as thus meeting and mingling together in a social capacity.

An application by the 10th Lanarkshire Rifle Volunteers to use the hall for drilling purposes was rejected.

Other business in those early days included setting the price to hire the upper hall; a *'concert or public meeting'* in the upper hall would cost three guineas for the evening while a *'concert, soiree and assembly'* would cost six guineas.

The health issues associated with smoking may not have uppermost in the minds of the trustees but they were very conscious that the interior of the building was almost entirely made of wood, so smoking was prohibited.

There must have been a few awkward encounters in the retiring rooms, i.e. the bathrooms, because an order was placed with a local signwriter to make signs for the doors to distinguish the gentlemen's room from the ladies' room.

A large building soon has to deal with the ingress of rainwater if drainage is not sufficient, so the hall keeper was kept busy in those early days dealing with leaks. As early as 1885, some parts of the roof had to be replaced because dry rot had become an issue.

After a few weeks, the trustees had to attend to complaints about the acoustics in the upper hall. The eminent gentlemen of the board went to the upper hall to investigate and decided that the cause of the poor acoustics was the open joints of the woodwork on the ceiling. Their solution was to fix crimson drugget, a heavy material over those joints.

William Dixon was a fierce protector of Govanhill and Crosshill's independence and for years had led resistance to efforts by the municipal authorities in Glasgow to absorb the area into the city. A shrewd businessman, he knew that annexation was highly likely and he stipulated in his gift of the hall that if the burghs ever submitted to Glasgow, then the Burgh Hall must be sold and profits given to any viable hospital that was established on the south side of the river.

Crosshill and Govanhill resisted Glasgow's advances for another 12 years, but in 1891 they bowed to the inevitable and the two burghs finally became part of the city. After intense negotiation the Burgh hall was sold to the city for £7,000 and the profits were given to the Victoria Infirmary.

What administrative function, if any, the halls served after annexation has been difficult to establish. What is certain is that it continued to be a venue for social events for many years.

In 1911, Dixon Halls is listed as the location for one of the first films ever to be shown in the district, though what that film was about or was called remains a mystery. In 1914, it was listed in a brochure published by Glasgow Corporation's Halls Department as having the capacity to accommodate 1,300 people at events, and at that time it also had a grand organ. Eventually the upper hall fell into disrepair and for many years was out of bounds, with only the ground floor halls in use.

In 1972, a lunch club started in the lower halls to counter the social isolation felt by many of the district's older residents, which soon became more ambitious, offering day care facilities and a programme of activities. What began as informal soon became formal and the lunch club became an official group called The Dixon Community who then successfully applied for a grant of £146,000 from Urban Aid. This grant allowed the renovation of the derelict upper hall and the provision of many new services: a dining room, television room, library and a games room, which the group still uses to this day.

A false ceiling hides the true size of the hall. The beams of the original ceiling can be seen if the tiles on the false ceiling are removed. There is probably space for two other floors above the current first floor. Above the reception desk on the first floor, a sloped ceiling indicates a small portion of the underside of the balcony that would once have surrounded the floor of the grand hall. The lower halls, the former courtrooms, are still used by The Dixon Community for a range of social activities.

Belleisle Street and Craigie Street Stations

Before the 1870s, there was neither a police force nor much in the way of public services in what would become Govanhill and Crosshill. Responsible citizens and businesses would carry out various civic duties but there was a degree of freedom on the south side of Glasgow that attracted many nefarious characters. Dubious enterprises and houses of ill-repute operated with impunity, just beyond the reaches of the law. Legitimate businesses also flourished in an environment with little regulation.

The General Police and Improvement Act of 1862 allowed communities with a population of 1,200 or more to become police burghs, which would empower them to apply for money from the government for municipal purposes. This was principally for improving streets, lighting and sanitation, but it also brought the protection of the county police force. Importantly, the Act allowed those burghs to remain independent of larger municipalities.

Crosshill became a police burgh in 1871 and Renfrew County Police assumed responsibility for policing in the area, but Govanhill's population had not yet exceeded 1,200, so it remained beyond the reach of both Glasgow's and Renfrew's police forces.

New tenements were being built rapidly in Govanhill in the 1870s and it was not long before the population had grown sufficiently. Both Crosshill and Glasgow wanted to annexe Govanhill and claim it as their own but in 1877 Govanhill became an independent police burgh in its own right.

In 1877, just after Govanhill became a burgh, William Smith Dixon, owner of the local iron works and most of the land in Govanhill and Crosshill, gifted the two burghs the magnificent municipal hall now known as Dixon Halls, completed in 1879. At the same time he enabled the building of a police and fire station on Belleisle Street, immediately behind Dixon Halls as well as accommodation for police officers in Belleisle House, named, like the street, after his summer residence in Ayr.

This building however, was for the sole use of the Govanhill Burgh. The Govanhill Police Force included two inspectors, three sub-inspectors, two sergeants and 28 constables.

On the 14th of May, 1879, the *North British Daily Mail* reported that:

In the opinion of Commander McHardy, Chief Constable of Lanarkshire, the new premises for police purposes just completed at Govanhill, and which is to be formally handed over to the keeping of the commissioners for the county tomorrow, is 'the finest police station in Scotland'.

The site, which covers about 1760 square yards in all , feud from W.S. Dixon, the well-known ironmaster, is at the south-east of the burgh, immediately contiguous to the fine Town Hall and Burgh buildings in course of construction for the joint use of Crosshill and Govanhill. The police station of which we are speaking, however, is for the sole use of the latter Burgh, Crosshill will require to provide for itself.

The new station, which is of two storeys with stables is in the old Scottish style of architecture, has a frontage of 50 feet, facing the west, and overlooking Belleisle Street, an unfinished thoroughfare running parallel with Cathcart Road, and which is to be as soon as possible completed, when it will connect Allison Street on the North with Dixon Avenue on the south.

At the surface level of the walls around the building is inserted a course of Caithness pavement, which will effectively prevent damp from rising and keep the walls above ground always dry. Entering by a couple of steps at the front centre door of the station, immediately on the left is the Lieutenant's room, at the counter of which he receives and takes record of all cases brought before him. It is a light and airy apartment, some 21 by 12 feet in dimensions, fitted up with every necessary convenience.

As we go in, a good fire is burning in a stove grate of somewhat superior appearance, and we learn that it is from here the cells are all comfortably warmed by means of hot-water pipe apparatus. At the northeast corner of the room is a door communicating with a nice little exercise yard or airing ground for prisoners. The floor of it asphalted, with a drainage arrangement for rain or other water at once to run away, and the walls are lined throughout with white enamelled bricks , which gives it a very light and cleanly appearance. Only one prisoner is allowed to use it at a time, and the construction of the place, with every corner being smoothed and rounded off and otherwise is such that there is not a coigne of vantage left to enable a cat to get over the wall.

The cells, each of which is as near as maybe a counterpart of the other, are four in number, and, beyond all question, are really 'on the most improved principle of construction', more especially in a sanitary point of view. They are each 11 by 8 feet, length and breadth, and 11 feet high, all the walls being like those of the airing yard lined with white enamelled bricks. Nowhere have we seen such ample and admirable arrangements for the purpose of ventilation as these cells exhibit. Each, it may be said has full ventilators – that is to say, ventilating apertures. One is at the bottom of one of the walls close to the floor, another is a movable slide at the top of the little window, a third is above the door, through which air comes from the corridor, and the fourth is in the centre of the roof. The current of air which ascends and goes up through the roof, its progress being accelerated by those coming from the door at the top of the window respectively. The cells are lighted by gas brackets outside in the corridor which latter is lighted by them as well.

The reason of the brackets being outside is that no prisoner in an unsafe state of mind should be able to make use of them to hang himself with. Everything, In short, about this lockup seems worthy of such commendation as the place received from Commander McHardy, and as regards those who may have perforce to become temporary sojourners within its walls, we cannot see – compatible with their being in distance at all – what they could wish for more.

The dwelling accommodation for constables upstairs, which we next briefly visit, consists of three houses for married men on the first floor, and two (for two single men) each, on the attic floor. All are excellent in their way, the rooms being unusually roomy and commanding from the windows and extensive and beautiful prospect.

Coming downstairs, we are pointed out at the rear of the building, a fine airy backyard for drying clothes, at one side of which is an excellent washing house, with capacious boiling copper, set in washing tubs. In addition to the police station proper, the buildings include a fire engine station, which forms a west wing of the station and includes a shed for the engine and another for the water cart, each 23 by 12 feet in dimensions, a tool house, 30 by 14 feet, and a spacious lamp house, for the use of both fire engine and police departments. Everything about the latter is, in its way, on a scale of equal efficiency with the arrangements of the lockup and the Burgh of Govanhill is to be congratulated on the possession of both at an early stage in its history.

Despite this glowing description of the building, other reports indicate that the first officers did not always reach the standards of professionalism required.

In the staff registers that were kept, there are a number of cases recorded of dismissal, with various reasons including:

Misconduct with servant girls on his beat.

Discharged for being drunk and differing with his neighbours.

Getting the worse of drink when on duty.

Frequently omitting to make daily entries in his duty book and evident unfitness for service.

Incivility of conduct.

Absent from his beat and late for duty. Dismissed for drunkenness.

False statement on his application.

In time, standards rose and fewer and fewer such cases were recorded.

In 1891, upon annexation, the City of Glasgow assumed responsibility for the district and Queen's Park or 'G' Division was created. Plans were drawn up for a new station to be built at Craigie Street, though the small station at Belleisle Street was still required. The station was visited regularly by an official from the Corporation who inspected the premises and recorded their findings in the visitors' book. The Superintendent was required to send a copy of the findings to the Chief Constable with any necessary report or explanation.

In 1897, one comment said the station was *'all right for ordinary matters. Dogs are kept in one place that is disgusting for men going in their hall. Fifteen dogs in one day. Smell abominable'*. Another report says simply *'dark and discreditable. Hall not clean'*. Clearly, the need for a new station was pressing. Crosshill did establish their own police and fire services, their activities were reported in the press, but information about where they were based, so far has proved elusive.

Craigie Street

In 1891, the City of Glasgow assumed responsibility for the district. Plans were drawn up for a new combined police and fire station to be built at Craigie Street, which would also include 40 apartments, to provide accommodation for officers, firemen and their families. There was a fire practice tower (which has long since been demolished) and even a 'hoist' which connected the ground floor to the other levels.

The new facility also included offices for the Lighting Department. The cost was projected to be £18,000, but final approval was delayed for some time by conservative members of the planning committee who considered the expense extravagant for a still, largely undeveloped area but approval was eventually granted. The precise opening date has been difficult to establish but the new station was open for business by late 1893.

The Police Station

One of the most notorious cases dealt with by 'G' Division became known as the 'Queen's Park Murder' in 1920. In February of that year, Henry Senior, a bachelor ex-soldier, who was injured in World War One, and lived in Robson Street with his widowed mother, met a prostitute called Helen Kennan on Hope Street. They boarded a tramcar for Mount Florida and then went to Queen's Park recreation ground. They agreed terms but then Kennan's boyfriend Albert Fraser, and his accomplice James Rollins, showed up and demanded money from Senior.

Rollins restrained Senior but he resisted, so Fraser pulled out a gun and beat him around the face, leaving him for dead. Fraser and Rollins then searched Senior's body; they even searched his boots but found less than 30 pence. Disappointed, they took his coat and boots and hid the body under some bushes.

The day after the murder, two schoolboys from the nearby Deaf and Dumb Institute, playing football in the park, found Senior's body and raised the alarm.

The investigation was led by Assistant Chief Constable Mennie, DCI Keith and DI Noble.

After appeals in the press for witnesses, a sharp-eyed tram conductor came forward and told police he had seen two men on the tram, one carrying a pair of boots. Enquiries at Central Station revealed the two men had boarded a train for Ardrossan, possibly bound for Belfast.

DCI Keith and DI Noble followed the trail to Belfast and apprehended Fraser and Rollins. Some reports say that they were caught near their lodgings and others claim they were found hiding out in a cave overlooking Belfast Lough.

At the trial in Glasgow, Fraser and Rollins were found guilty and were sentenced to death by hanging. Appeals to commute the sentences to life imprisonment were denied. The execution took place on 26th May 1920, the last double hanging to take place in Scotland, but not the last murder case the Queen's Park Division ever had to deal with.

Another notorious case was the Allison Street Murders in 1969. Howard Wilson joined Glasgow Police Force in 1958 and worked out of the station at Craigie Street. Wilson was ambitious but left the police force in 1968 because he believed he was not being promoted quickly enough. There were rumours that he had been involved in a bribery scandal a few years earlier, which may have hindered his advancement.

After leaving the force he set up a greengrocer's business in Govanhill but it was unsuccessful and he soon found himself heavily in debt.

Wilson, along with another former policeman, John Sim, and their childhood friend Ian Donaldson, were members of Bearsden Gun Club. All three men were having financial difficulties and after a drunken night spent playing cards, they joked that what they needed to do was rob a bank. But as their financial predicaments deepened, that drunken joke turned into a serious plan. In July 1969, they robbed the British Linen Bank in Giffnock, escaping with £21,000.

Emboldened by their success, a few months later they robbed the Clydesdale Bank in Bridge Street, Linwood, escaping with £14,000. In what would prove to be a foolish move, they returned to Wilson's flat in Allison Street, just opposite the rear entrance to the station where Wilson had once worked.

A former colleague, Inspector Andrew Hyslop, spotted Wilson and his two colleagues entering their building, carrying large cases. Hyslop recognised his former colleague and having long suspected Wilson of criminal activity, he summoned three other officers to assist in making an impromptu search of Wilson's flat.

When the police officers entered the flat, they were confronted with a wide-eyed Wilson brandishing a gun. Constable Barrett and Inspector McKenzie were shot and died on the scene. Constable Sellars barricaded himself in the bathroom and radioed for help. Inspector Hyslop suffered horrific facial injuries and would have died on the scene if Wilson's gun had not jammed.

Wilson was sentenced to life with a recommendation that he serve at least 25 years. His accomplices Sim and Donaldson, who had played no part in the shooting, were sentenced to 12 years. Wilson was eventually released in 2002.

The Fire Station

The fire station was part of the same complex as the police station but the main frontage was on Allison Street. Firemen and their families lived on site. Catriona Stewart, talking in 1986, recalls her childhood growing up in the station:

> I feel privileged to have been brought up in Queen's Park Fire Station, learning the true values in life, respect for each other, love and a sense of service to others. Certainly, the men my dad worked with were the salt of the earth.

Catriona recalls how the fire service was a respected profession and when she mentioned her father's profession at school, other children would be envious.

During World War Two, there was blast-proof shelter in the centre of the building and while sheltering there during one raid, Catriona and her mother heard a loud blast and thought the fire station had been hit but the bomb had fallen on Deanston Drive, half a mile away.

One day, while all the engines were away on call, the chip pan in Catriona's kitchen caught fire. Her mother had no option but to call Gorbals fire station and ask them to attend. By the time the fire engines from the Gorbals had arrived, her mother had extinguished the fire but the men from the Gorbals fire service never let the men from Queen's Park forget that they had to come to the rescue.

Firemen were on six days out of seven and, when not on call, would be cleaning, polishing or scrubbing the vehicles or equipment.

Today, Belleisle Street station is still standing, but since 1979 it has been a boxing club. Belleisle House, next door, where police officers lived in the 1870s and 1880s, was, until recently, a care home run by the Dixon Community.

The fire and police stations at Craigie Street and Allison Street remained in operation until 1986 and for the most part have been converted to housing. There is still a small police office within the complex on Craigie Street, which is open for a few hours each week.

Queen's Park United Presbyterian Church

In the 1860s, the United Presbyterian faith was the largest denomination in Glasgow. The inhabitants of the new district of Crosshill wanted easier access to a church, so a 'preaching station', a simple wooden house, was opened in October 1866 and the first service was led by Reverend Doctor Eadie, Reverend Doctor Young of Glasgow and Reverend William Sprott from Pollokshaws. A few months later a congregation was formed and Reverend Sprott was inducted in May 1867.

The new congregation soon decided that a larger building was required; a committee was formed and renowned architect Alexander 'Greek' Thompson's plan was accepted. Thompson had already built three other churches in Glasgow. The new church would cost £7,000 and would accommodate 1,200 people. The church opened in May 1869.

In *The Historical Notices of the United Presbyterian Congregations in Glasgow* J. Logan Aikman describes the church in the following way:

Besides the ordinary galleries at each side and one end there is a gallery behind the platform and a second-tier opposite. The artificial lighting is peculiar. The platform is lighted by candelabra but the body of the church by jets, projecting, at intervals of seven inches, from piping laid on two sides and one end along the entablature. The interior finishing is only of wood, no plaster whatever in any part of the building and, with the exception of an ornament over each door to the platform there is no carving.

The decoration is obtained by design in colour from drawings by the architect. The effect of the interior is rich and harmonious, and is amongst the best expressions on this country of the spirit of Greek art. Externally, from the dignity of the composite and the exquisite beauty of the details, no less than the originality of the design, this church is eminently noteworthy among the public buildings of Glasgow.

The church took its mission to serve the community and district seriously. This included missionary work in the village of Strathbungo, a Sunday evening school often catering for over 100 scholars, a sewing class for 30 girls, and a savings bank. They also held a morning meeting at the Govan Colliery and supported the Govan Colliery School, which in 1873 had 831 scholars and 81 teachers.

In 1900, the congregation joined with the Free Church and was known as Queen's Park East United Free Church of Scotland. In 1929, it became known as Queen's Park St. Georges.

On 25th March 1943, during one of the last ever German bombing raids in Glasgow, the church was hit by an incendiary bomb and rapidly burned to the ground.

However, due to wartime reporting restrictions, the press was not allowed to identify the church. A report in the *Glasgow Herald* on 26th March, said simply: *'This church was destroyed by incendiaries during yesterday morning's raid on a town in Central Scotland'*.

Crosshill Synagogue

There has been a Jewish community in Govanhill and Crosshill since the early 20th century. In 1901, a *chevra*, or prayer group, met in a baker's shop on Langside Road, later moving to Cromwell Road (which would become Niddrie Road) and opening a new synagogue. Over the years, there have been tailors, delicatessens, newsagents and many other small businesses with a Jewish connection.

On 20th September 1933, the *Evening Times* reported:

A recent influx of Jews into the Crosshill District has led to the formation of still another Hebrew Congregation and the new synagogue premises were opened only this week for the Festival services. The new synagogue which seats over a hundred is situated in Dixon Avenue and was formerly the Home for Aged and Needy Jews which opened in 1927.

The house at 61 Dixon Avenue was purchased for £200 by a group led by Robert Sharmutze, who considered the membership fees of established synagogues in the area too high. The Crosshill Synagogue became known locally as 'a cut-price shul' because the membership had a higher proportion of small businessmen and traders, as well as artisans and craft workers, than other synagogues. Though, when occasion demanded, larger, more sacred services and events would be held at Dixon Halls.

Over time, the house on Dixon Avenue became unsafe, no longer fit for purpose and as no seating was available in the other local synagogues, the need for a new place of worship was pressing. In 1955, now led by the charismatic Polish Rabbi, Moses Drynan, a building fund was established and the search began for new premises.

Eventually, a site was identified on Belleisle Street and the foundation stone was laid on Sunday 1st May 1960 by Sir Maurice Bloch, distiller and philanthropist, and the building finally opened in 1961. Like the 'cut-price shul' on Dixon Avenue, the Belleisle Street Synagogue was a modest, functional building compared to other more lavish synagogues in the neighbourhood, but it still served a vital and important function for its congregation. Israel Brodie, Chief Rabbi of Great Britain at the time, praised the work of local young people:

the building of synagogues and centres for the religious instruction of the children and for social and cultural activities has ever been the first and sacred duty of a community of Jews, wherever their lot was cast.

There was seating for 470 and plans were made to build a gallery. *The Citizen* reported that the new synagogue would be *'home to many who have deserted Gorbals and have made their homes in Allison Street'*. From time to time, Dixon Halls would still be used for larger services. The new premises was not just a venue for services but for a wide range of social activities, friendship groups and Hebrew classes. Manny Shinwell, Labour MP and former Red Clydesider, was the Honorary Secretary of the congregation.

In 1963, in a move that indicates the growing confidence of the congregation, a then unknown artist called Alasdair Gray was commissioned to paint a mural on the ceiling of the synagogue. President of the congregation, Alex Rosenthal, said after its unveiling:

we hadn't actually contemplated having the ceiling decorated but when it was finished we were very pleased with it. The painting harmonises with the contemporary design of the synagogue and it has excited favourable comments from visitors.

Rabbi Drynan died in 1978 and that proved a watershed moment for the congregation; many had already moved further south to Giffnock and Newton Mearns and numbers were steadily declining. A new rabbi was brought in from France to lead for a while but many of the older congregation could not adjust to the change.

There were many heated discussions about what to do next but it was eventually decided to merge with the Queen's Park Congregation. The final service at Crosshill Synagogue was held in November 1986.

The former synagogue on Belleisle Street is now a community drop-in centre called The Space.

Govanhill Socialist Sunday School

The Govanhill Socialist Sunday School was not based in a special long-lost building but is included here because the story of that school has not been widely told.

The Socialist Sunday School movement began in Glasgow in the 1890s, under the guidance of Keir Hardie, chairman of the Independent Labour Party. The schools were created to teach socialist values and offer an alternative to lessons being taught in state schools and churches. Glasgow, with its strong industrial base and tradition of labour activism, was the perfect city in which to start the movement and within a few years there were 15 branches in Glasgow, and many more across the country.

Keir Hardie wrote:

We need to teach children the first principles of socialism. Our movement can make a contribution to the cause of peace and socialism, work for a better way of life for the children of all lands.

Many members still attended conventional churches but the Socialist Sunday Schools were designed to encourage young people (and their parents) to stand up for themselves, to learn to speak in public, to teach socialist values, and to encourage some of them to become activists in the future. The schools were as much, if not more, about building character than they were about teaching ideology.

As in conventional religion, there were ten commandments, but with a slightly different emphasis, the new directives were a combination of Socialism and Christianity:

1. Love your schoolfellows, who will be your fellow workmen in life.

2. Love learning, which is the food of the mind. Be as grateful to your teacher as to your parents.

3. Make every day holy by good and useful deeds and kindly actions.

4. Honour the good, be courteous to all, bow down to none.

5. Do not hate or speak evil of anyone. Do not be revengeful but stand up for your rights and resist oppression.

6. Do not be cowardly, be a friend to the weak, and love justice.

7. Remember that the good things of the earth are produced by labour. Whoever enjoys them without working for them is stealing the bread of the workers.

8. Observe and think in order to discover the truth. Do not believe what is contrary to reason and never deceive yourself or others.

9. Do not think that those who love their own country must hate and despise other nations, or wish for war, which is a remnant of barbarism.

10. Work for the day when all men and women will be free citizens of one fatherland and live together as brothers and sisters in peace and righteousness.

Singing socialist hymns was also part of the Sunday School experience; school leaders were determined to show that God did not have all the best tunes. Most meetings would finish with a rendition of *The Red Flag* or *The Internationale.*

The *Young Socialist* magazine was the organ of the Sunday School movement. In February 1925, William Moran wrote that:

> I am strongly of the opinion that so long as the adult's movement ignores the children's movement as it so often does, the latter will never make the progress it otherwise might. The capitalists teach the children from birth to support the present system – and we allow them to do so. Progress for the working-class movement cannot be hoped for in these circumstances. Remember, it is the duty of every socialist to send his children to Sunday School.

Many schools faced opposition from conventional churches and society at large and were often turned away by hall keepers when they tried to book space for a meeting. A number of people believed the schools indoctrinated children with Marxist ideas and encouraged revolution. Gradually, the schools began to earn respect from more liberal-minded church leaders.

Reverend White, at a meeting of the Glasgow Presbytery in 1921, said:

> The Church has never yet taken its stand against the owning classes of the country. It has supported wars and forgotten the teaching of him who preached love and not hate when any minister of the church, as happened locally, had the courage to preach Christ and not capital, they were crucified by their own congregation. It was for the Church to get away from the idea that the condition from which the masses were suffering today was the result of divine will.

Meetings would include storytelling sessions with fairy tale characters or popular children's characters such as Brer Rabbit, and there was always a good socialist value built into the story.

Collections were made to help striking workers in Dublin, or wherever current industrial action or humanitarian relief demanded. Other recipients included the Russian Orphan Fund or the Russian Famine Relief Fund.

Sessions would often include a 'new born' ceremony, which was a little like a christening in a church but the new arrivals would be welcomed into the arms of socialism and parents would pledge to raise their child accordingly.

Children were also encouraged to perform 'items'; short songs, poems or stories according to their talents or abilities. In the pre-war era, before radio or television, everyone was expected to contribute to domestic entertainment, so children often already had an item to perform or were encouraged at the school to create one.

In the meetings, children would also learn the rules of committee behaviour. Motions would be made, often motivated by or inspired by issues of the day, and then voted on, and minutes of those debates and resolutions would often be taken by the children themselves.

Simple lessons would be taught to encourage solidarity. For instance, teachers would demonstrate that two or three matches could be easily snapped but a whole boxful of matches could not be so easily broken.

Slightly more advanced lessons on helpfulness included the important message that *'boys ought not to be ashamed of anything to lighten the burden of their mothers and sisters'*. Poems were composed to reinforce a lesson, such as:

> *And we practice as we go*
> *On the little things we meet*
> *Carrying Granny's parcel for her*
> *Guiding blind men o'er the street*
> *Lifting up a fallen baby*
> *Helping mother all we may*

For the very young children there was the Sunbeam Club, modelled after nurseries in Russia.

In January 1909, the *Young Socialist* magazine proudly announced that a new school would open that month in Govanhill:

> A new school will be opened on the second Sunday in January. Place of meeting Dixon Halls, Cathcart Road. Time 3pm. All comrades and sympathisers cordially invited and expected. Be sure to send the children.

The first meeting was conducted by Comrade Alfred Russell. Comrade Jim Hamilton gave a lesson entitled *Socialist Jack and The Beanstalk*.

Secretary Maggy Cree also records that there was a pianoforte solo from Miss Westwater and a solo from Miss Whyte, which helped make the first meeting a great success.

The core lesson of the text of the first meeting was that *'All men, women and children have but one need in common, the need of living and being happy'*.

Thirty-six children along with 56 adults attended the first meeting. Over the coming weeks attendances would rise steadily.

Maggy Cree reported later in the year that:

> we have appointed a small committee of children to visit the attached and unattached socialists in the district with an effort to increase the sale of our Young Socialist magazine.

Later meetings of the Govanhill school are recorded as being held at the Independent Labour Rooms at 100 Batson Street.

The Independent Labour Party flourished until the 1930s, but with its decline attendances at the schools were much lower, though the Glasgow schools remained active.

After World War Two, attendances declined again. With the election of a Labour government and the promise of a national health service, many felt that a fairer society was about to be realised.

The school at Govanhill almost closed in 1945 but was revitalised briefly with a few naming ceremonies. However, by 1956, with only 13 members it was impossible to keep going. The school received this letter from the Glasgow Secretary:

> Dear Comrade, I am sorry to hear that Govanhill Socialist Sunday School has had to close but I can understand how much you have tried to keep the school going. You keep going until it is impossible to carry on any longer.
>
> Yours in comradeship
>
> May Gibson

Despite valiant efforts to reignite interest and start again, the school closed in November of 1956.

One former member recalled:

> If everyone lived up to the things they're taught at Socialist Sunday School, they'd have turned out to be good adults. It was a good thing, the Socialist Sunday School, it let you see things, it let you hear things. I think it gave me the foundation of what I am today. And often I'll remember wee quotes –

> *The children are the nation's heirs*
> *And we are certain quite*
> *The fullness of the earth is theirs*
> *If they had but the right.*
> *For this we'll fight, for this we'll pray*
> *For this we'll labour every day!*

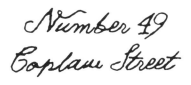

The Air Force Auxiliary

In 1925 the Air Force Auxiliary was instituted and the following year the first squadrons were formed. A base was built on the corner of Coplaw Street, on the west side of Victoria Road, next to the older drill hall that originally belonged to Third Lanarkshire Rifle Volunteers.

The premises were formally opened on the 12th of July by King George V and Queen Mary, who were in Glasgow for just one day, during which they also opened the Kelvin Hall and the George V Bridge on Oswald Street. Traffic came to a standstill around Coplaw Street as the royal couple arrived, welcomed by a guard of honour and three planes belonging to the squadron circled overhead. They were only in the new building for 30 minutes but were invited to inspect the squadron's collection of parachutes, Lewis guns, incendiary bombs and larger, 1600lb bombs.

The Air Force Auxiliary provided reinforcements for the Royal Air Force and consisted of paid volunteers who would give some of their evenings, weekends and holidays to train at the new base at nearby Renfrew Airport. The volunteers generally came from the wealthier sections of society as applicants were expected to already have, or be prepared to obtain, their pilot's licence at their own expense, at a cost of £96 (about £5,000 in today's money). All serving members were required to wear the letter 'A' on their uniforms.

On the ground floor at Coplaw Street was an orderly room, an adjutant's room, a sergeant's room, a tech annexe, a tech store, a lecture room and a large drill hall. Upstairs were bedrooms, living rooms, an officer's room, a dressing room and a balcony overlooking the drill hall.

During World War Two, the Air Force Auxiliary was embodied, or incorporated, into the Royal Air Force and subsequently became known as the 602 (City of Glasgow) Squadron. They were equipped with Hurricanes and Spitfires, notably shooting down some of the first enemy bombers flying over Britain. The squadron was heavily involved during the evacuation of troops from Dunkirk and the Battle of Britain. After the war ended, the 20 squadrons of the Air Force Auxiliary were honoured with the prefix Royal and continued to serve with distinction, particularly during the Berlin Air Lift between 1948 and 1949 and the Korean War during the 1950s. A Spitfire from the

602 Squadron now hangs majestically in the Kelvingrove Art Gallery in Glasgow.

The Air Force Cadets, formed in 1941, would also come to drill and train at Coplaw Street after the war. In 1957, the Royal Air Force Auxiliary was disbanded and amalgamated into other squadrons. The 602 Squadron became part of 603 Squadron based in Edinburgh. After lying derelict for a few years, the building on Coplaw Street was taken over by the Jewish Board of Guardians who were relocating from the Gorbals. In 2006, the 602 Squadron was reformed as a general support unit.

The Jewish Board of Guardians

The Jewish Board of Guardians formed in 1867 and was originally based in Thistle Street in the Gorbals but by the late 1960s that building was no longer fit for purpose; at the same time, the Jewish community was moving further south to Queen's Park, Langside, Crosshill and Govanhill so new premises were required. Not long after this, the Guardians moved to 49 Coplaw Street and they changed their name to the Glasgow Jewish Welfare Board. The Board's remit was *'the coordination and centralisation of communal welfare activities'* and to further that goal, they leased space at Coplaw Street to a number of organisations serving the Jewish community.

The Jewish Blind Society

The Jewish Blind Society made their base at Coplaw Street. Their objective was to look after blind and partially sighted members in conjunction with the Welfare Board. The Blind Society enabled its members to escape from the restrictions of their disabilities and to live richer, fuller lives. Services included a lunch club twice a week, meals on wheels, help obtaining essential everyday items or organising day trips or longer holidays. Core funding was provided by subscribers contributing various amounts on a regular basis. Accounts show that contributions varied from £1 a month to £100 a month.

The Avrom Greenbaum Players

The Glasgow Jewish Institute Players, formed in 1936 by Avrom Greenbaum, would become one of the most influential community theatre groups in Scotland. In 1936, the group was based at the Jewish Institute in South Portland Street in the Gorbals and performed in The Bloch Theatre. Greenbaum was an inspirational director and playwright who combined his commitment to theatre with a full-time job in his family's tailoring business.

Greenbaum's group was one of four left-leaning theatre companies who would occasionally collaborate under the banner of Glasgow Unity Theatre. The other groups were the Worker's Theatre Group, the Clarion players, and The Transport Players.

The Jewish Institute Players were distinctive for high production standards and an ambitious repertoire, often exploring Jewish identity, history and culture, with some of the plays written by Greenbaum himself.

Many performers who started in the group would go on to enjoy professional careers, such as Ida Schuster, Sam and Harry Hankin, Bonita Beach, Joe Boyers, and Kalman Glass.

After Greenbaum's death in 1963, the group took on the name of their founder and were known thereafter as the Avrom Greenbaum Players. By 1970, the Jewish Institute was in a poor state of repair, so the group followed many in the Jewish community south of the river and took up residence in Coplaw Street. Fortunately, they were able to convert the old drill hall into a purpose-built theatre, constructed exactly to their requirements. The initials AG were proudly emblazoned on the new stage curtains.

The repertoire was still ambitious, probably more varied than in Greenbaum's day, and included not just straight plays, but musicals, comedies and many charity events.

The group would stage two to three productions a year at Coplaw Street. The first production there was Tango by Slawomir Mrozek followed by a musical called The Fantasticks by Tom Jones and Harvey Schmidt.

The group did not just perform in Coplaw Street but regularly entered competitions run by Scottish Community Drama Association, winning the annual festival in 1976 with their production of *Who's Afraid of Virginia Woolf?*

In the late summer every year a notice would appear in the local press inviting locals to audition at *'The Theatre'* in Coplaw Street. All were welcome to try out.

By 1990, it was proving harder to attract new members, many in the Jewish community had moved further south in the city and the building at Coplaw Street was in a poor state of repair. The last production by the Avrom Greenbaum Players and the last play to be performed at Coplaw Street was Brighton Beach Memoirs by Neil Simon in 1991.

Number 49 also played host to the *Jewish Echo*, a weekly newspaper (later renamed *The Jewish Times*), as well as the Jewish Representative Council and a kosher restaurant.

In 1996, the building closed and the surviving groups relocated. The Welfare Board is now known as Jewish Care Scotland and based in Giffnock.

The building at 49 Coplaw Street was demolished and in 2001 new housing opened on the site.

The Drill Hall on Coplaw Street: Third Lanark Rifle Volunteers

French military expansion in the 1850s caused a fear of war across the country. Poet Laureate, Alfred Tennyson famously urged the country to take up arms with the line *'Form! Form! Riflemen form!'* and soon the government yielded to the demand of the people to be armed.

The Third Lanark Rifle Volunteers were formed from a combination of several older, independent units, including the 8th Coy Etna Foundry and the remnants of the 78th Corps Old Guard of Glasgow.

There was no Coplaw Street in 1859, but the new company set up base just south of Coplawhill Nursery in makeshift buildings and conducted drills and parades locally.

As part of army reforms in 1881, the four Lanarkshire Volunteer regiments were attached to the newly formed Cameronians, informally known as The Scottish Rifles. Further legislation followed and in 1884, the Regulation of The Forces Act gave regiments the right to acquire land and apply for grants to build drill halls. The largest period of drill hall construction took place between 1884 and 1910.

In April 1884, the *British Architect* journal announced *'operations have commenced to construct a new drill hall and headquarters at Coplawhill. The architect is James Bennie Wilson, one of the officers of the regiment'*.

It is believed that the Bennie family owned property at Coplawhill, so acquisition of land for the hall on the recently formed Coplaw Street was probably straightforward.

The new drill hall was 142 feet long, 72 feet wide. A single span roof left the floor free of any obstruction. The interior walls were made with white enamelled bricks relieved with coloured bands.

At the time, there were no other halls in the immediate vicinity suitable for large public meetings, so it was hoped that the new hall would meet that requirement and provide accommodation for the regiment. The building included many other rooms for the different ranks in the regiment, an armoury and a gymnasium. The total cost of construction was £4,000.

In 1889, the drill hall was the venue for the Annual Children's Ball, organised by a local teacher called Robert Sellars. Two hundred children assembled at Queen's Park one Saturday afternoon and then marched to the hall. A journalist in attendance wrote that:

> The spectators' sitting and standing room was filled to see little maidens in dainty frocks, magnificent sashes, silk stockings and tiny slippers and small boys in kilts, Eton suits and white waistcoats. It was a caution to see the children take their partner's hand with all the gallantry of a 17th century courtier. Mamas and papas wept with pride. The Ball was a great success and broke up at 10 o'clock.

In 1894, one member of the regiment, a Private Rennie, completed in the Bisley Tournament, a shooting competition in London and won the title of 'Queen's Prizeman', basically, the top marksman in the country that year, and he was afforded a hero's welcome when he returned to Glasgow. Thousands lined the street between Central Station and Coplaw Street to get a glimpse of the conquering hero. In 1898, another member of the regiment Lieutenant David Yates won the same prize and was similarly feted when he returned to Glasgow.

In 1904, the hall was extended and some of the original parts of the building were taken down. In 1908, the regiment was renamed the Seventh Battalion of the Cameronians and the Third Lanarkshire Rifle Volunteers were no more.

Operations continued at Coplaw Street and during the Great War, and there was even a number of recruiting concerts held there, one in particular, was led by the great Harry Lauder, the great Scots entertainer.

On the continent, the new regiment were in the thick of the action, and fought at Gallipoli and the Western front, suffering massive casualties.

After 1918, the hall was used regularly for sports such as boxing, badminton and gymnastics, and in 1947, after the second war, there was even an exhibition of equipment used in beach landings. The hall also played host to the annual regimental reunion dinner every year, until 1967, when the regiment was finally disbanded and the hall closed.

The drill hall was eventually demolished, but in 1984, the rest of the building, the offices and residential block, were converted to a leisure centre and achieved listed status in 1992. In 2001, the entire building was converted to apartments.

One of a series of local history articles published in the *Southside Press* in 1914, indicate that the very first school in the area, funded by William Dixon, for the children of his colliery workers, came into operation in the early 19th century in Butterbiggins Cottage on Butterbiggins Road.

In those early days, there was little in the way of educational provision locally, even the churches had yet to fully establish themselves in the area, so for most children living in and around the colliery, a basic education was not easy to achieve.

Dixon would have been aware of a historic obligation on landowners to provide some schooling to local children, but he would have also seen that service as a way to attract more workers to his domain, beyond the boundaries of the city.

The very first school was the porter's lodge for Larkfield House, situated on Butterbiggins Road, but within a few years that building would prove too small for its intended purpose, and so sometime in the 1810s, Dixon, along with others, provided a purpose-built venue that became known as the Govan Colliery School. The location of the school was approximately where Cathcart Road meets Coplaw Street today.

On the opening day of this new seat of learning, there was a celebration, during which Dixon, wearing his distinctive, swallow-tailed coat, his supervisor and some of his workers, danced with the locals while the colliery band played.

Although intended initially for the children of colliery workers, as the local population grew and diversified, more children attended the school, even from neighbouring districts, and all of them would have to pay a fee for lessons, which would provide the schoolmaster, or dominie, with a wage. The dominie was also provided with a house, this house was called Hayfield House and it stood on the corner of Butterbiggins Road, a short walk from the school. Hayfield is probably an indication that there was at that time, still lots of agricultural activity in the area.

The school did provide a good standard of education. An inspection by the Govan Parish Board, in 1856, reported:

> We, the undersigned, having this day examined the Govan Colliery School, at great length, desire hereby

to express ourselves as being highly satisfied with the attainments of the scholars, under the tuition of Mr Neilson and his assistant Mr MacMun and our rich appreciation of the advantage of such an institution for the neighbourhood.

One distinguished pupil was Fred Lamond, who would go on to become one of Scotland and Britain's most celebrated classical pianists in the late 19th and early 20th century.

Some of the older, more academically inclined pupils, would become pupil-teachers and then go onto full careers in education. Some former pupils took up careers in local government and business, and many others would find employment in the local colliery or iron works.

On one occasion though (at least one occasion) the temptations of a nearby swimming pond proved too much to resist for some pupils one lunchtime. The *Southside Press* reported:

When the pupils were all bathing in the swim pond when the whistle blew, they were, of course, naked and could not return to school. The master came down to the pond and the boys waded to an island with their clothing above their heads. The master had to go without them that afternoon. When the clothes were on, they were afraid, being long after the hour, to go to school. The next morning, they were rowed out on the floor to be strapped.

The school also became something of a community hub, providing space for a Sunday school, evening classes for adults and local events.

One weekend in 1867, there was a major flower show at the Victoria Gardens, on the opposite side of Cathcart Road. There were over 5,000 people in attendance, entertained by a pipe band and the school was taken over for additional floral displays and for the prizegiving ceremony. The upper floor of the school also for a while, housed the Govan Colliery Library.

Everything changed with the Education Act of 1872 which introduced compulsory education, but it would be three years before the first public school opened on Calder Street. The Colliery School continued, under the auspices of the Govan School Board, to provide classes until the new building opened.

Sometime after that transition was made, it was taken over by the Govanhill Evangelical Union and served as a place of worship and a Sunday School for a few more years but was demolished in the early 1890s, to make way for new housing.

The Govan Colliery School would be remembered by many who attended, as the Auld Brick School; because when it was built, and for many years afterwards, it was the only brick building in the area, it was also remembered for its distinctive, sloping roof, probably an indication of its dilapidated condition later in its life, rather than an original design feature.

The Drill Hall on Butterbiggins Road: First Lanarkshire Volunteer Artillery

The drill hall on Butterbiggins Road was never as grand nor as architecturally significant as the nearby Coplaw Street drill hall, but served ordinary soldiers more than well-to-do officers.

The Lord Provost of Glasgow opened the new hall on 18th January 1902. This was one of four halls across the city, designed to make it easier for members to attend.

One hundred and ten feet long and 50 feet wide, the new drill hall had a 'Belfast' roof of corrugated iron and wood. There were several other rooms for the business of the regiment, including accommodation.

The Provost said he hoped that by opening the hall, it showed that Glasgow was ready to assume responsibility for defence of the country.

Led by Colonel Dobie, the regiment hoped to train in the use of firearms and larger guns, when they could get them, and would also train in the care, riding, driving and manoeuvring of horses.

The regiment fought in Gallipoli and Palestine during the Great War. In 1908, they were subsumed into the Territorial Army. During World War Two, they fought in Normandy and North West Europe.

After the war, the territorials continued to use the hall on Butterbiggins Road until 1961.

The hall lay derelict for many years and was finally demolished in 2021 to make way for new housing. Initially, the developers talked about preserving the carved sign from above the entrance to the Drill Hall, with the regiment's name, and incorporating it into new housing but at the time of writing, that outcome has not yet been achieved.

Calder Street School

In 1866, a government inquiry led by the Duke of Argyll discovered that although the education system in Scotland compared favourably to that in England, still nearly half of all children were receiving no education at all. This led to the Education Act of 1872, which would subsequently lead to the building of hundreds of new schools. Attendance was made compulsory for all five- to 13-year-olds, and poverty would no longer be accepted as an excuse for truancy.

To implement this plan, the Act created and empowered 1,000 school boards across the country, including Govan School Board, which was given responsibility for education within the Parish of Govan. The Parish covered a vast area on both the south side and the north side of the River Clyde. On the north side it included Partick, and on the south side, it stretched, almost from Rutherglen in the east to Renfrew in the west. The area that would become Govanhill had always been part of the Parish of Govan.

Work started in 1874, to build 11 new schools within the parish, Calder Street School was the fourth school to be built, and at the time, it would be the second largest of those new schools, designed to accommodate 860 pupils. The opening ceremony, officiated by Mr Stephen, the chairman of the Govan School Board, took place on the 28th of September 1875.

Reports are unclear, but the design of the school is commonly attributed to an architectural company called Clark and Bell, based on St. Vincent Street, who designed a distinctive building in a Jacobean revival style, with crow-stepped gables and two pairs of spiral chimneys.

In 1879, the school achieved a pass rate of 96.2% and the accompanying report, included the comment *'efficient and satisfactory'*.

As the population of Govanhill increased, particularly in the 1880s, the school would have had to deal with more and more pupils, and with only one school in the area, this led to the mixing of pupils from working-class families, with children from middle-class families.

In order to alleviate the problem of overcrowding, there was a proposal put forward at a school board meeting, to build an extension at the Calder Street School, but it was pointed out by one of the board members, that this would not solve the problem of the mixing of the *'different castes'*.

One journalist tried to explain the concerns of those parents and revealed just how class-ridden Victorian society was, and just how closely the different classes lived together in Govanhill. Apparently, the parents middle-class children were concerned not just about overcrowding but the effect on their offspring, of having to mix with the lower classes:

> in case it would lower their dignity or contaminate their children's character, would not allow them to mix with the commonality that attended the Calder Street School and therefore send them to another to receive their education at a more genteel school.

This led to the parents of pupils from Govanhill's more prosperous West Ward, encompassing the area between Victoria Road and Langside Road, withdrawing their children from Calder Street School and sending them instead to another school in the more prosperous area of Pollokshields.

Inevitably, the school at Pollokshields soon became overcrowded and Govan School Board were compelled to make plans to build a new school in the area, which would open the following year on Annette Street.

A few years later the school again had to contend with public opinion, but this time it was not the parents who sought change but the pupils themselves. The boys of the 4th, 5th and 6th grade went on strike against the long hours of the school day and the recent imposition of home lessons or homework. They were joined by pupils from the nearby Govanhill Public School on Annette Street and from a school in Polmadie, and together they spent an afternoon marching round other schools on the south side, protesting their case.

This was not an isolated incident, there were similar actions across Scotland what one journalist called *'the schoolboy strike epidemic'*. Fortunately for the militant pupils the staff at Calder Street School took an indulgent view of the disruption and when some of the pupils returned later that afternoon, tired and penitent, no more was said on the matter. Other pupils took the rest of the day off and did not return until the following morning. Whether they faced any consequences for their absence is unknown.

Educational reforms after World War One, meant that Calder Street School, in common with many other schools in Scotland, also became a junior secondary. After finishing the primary stage, pupils would either continue at Calder Street for up to three years, taking commercial or vocational courses, while those with academic inclinations would transfer to Queen's Park Secondary.

The school continued to function as a primary and a junior secondary until 1967, but at that point in Glasgow's history, comprehensive redevelopment was the dominant ideology amongst Glasgow's planners, which led to the demolition of many tenements in the Gorbals, and to many new families moving into Govanhill and Crosshill. This upsurge in the local population required many pupils being assigned to other schools. Pupils from Calder Street School were transferred to Victoria Primary on Govanhill Street and to other schools in the area, while Calder Street School itself became an annexe of Holy Cross Primary, a Roman Catholic school, on the opposite side of Calder Street.

In more recent years, the school has served some new social and community purposes, such as a base for the Al-Falaah Mosque and a number of social work projects, including AMINA and REACH who worked closely with the BME community locally. Those latter projects have since moved onto new locations, but the mosque remains and there is also a successful nursery school, maintaining a meaningful link to the building's educational origins.

Crosshill House

After the Reformation in 1564, the Lands of Crosshill were feud to Sir John Minto, who was then Provost of Glasgow. He built what was probably the first Crosshill House in 1587, located on what is now Crosshill Avenue, but after he passed the house and the lands changed hands several times.

In 1642, Gabriel Thomson took possession, and the Thomson family presided in Crosshill for over a century.

In 1739, the old house was demolished, and a new two-storey house was built which contained a large garden, a sunken orchard, and a vinery. The house faced east along a tree-lined route to Cathcart Road.

William Rowan of Bellahouston, nephew of the last of the Thompsons, acquired Crosshill in 1782. He died in 1784 and the house was inherited by his son James, and later his younger son Thomas.

In 1812, Thomas sold the 64-acre estate, the seven-roomed house, and the freestone quarry to Robert Clark, who lived there until 1845. The indication of a nearby quarry is a clue that there was a village in Crosshill long before there were any villas. An 1851 report talks about a village of Crosshill with sixty-three inhabitants, east of Cathcart Road, next to a quarry:

a village, in the parish of Cathcart, Upper ward of the county of Renfrew, two miles south of from Glasgow; containing sixty-three inhabitants. It lies in the northern part of the parish, and on the east-ern confines of the county; the road from Glasgow to Cathcart runs a short distance westward of the village. There is a valuable quarry of freestone, which is extensively wrought for the erection of buildings in Glasgow.

Robert Clark's trustees sold the house and the lands of Crosshill to William Dixon in 1845. Crosshill, by this time was an irregular shaped piece of land between Cathcart Road on the east and Pollokshaws Road on the west. The northern boundary of Crosshill was what would later become Dixon Avenue and the southern boundary would later become Queen's Drive.

The next resident of Crosshill House was William Wilson, who owned the Lilybank Boiler works at Tollcross – he lived in Crosshill House until the 1860s.

Crosshill became an independent, self-governing burgh on the 5th of September 1871, there were just five streets at the time. One hundred and nineteen people voted in favour and sixty-four voted against the motion of becoming a burgh.

Another notable resident of Crosshill House was John Robertson, he was clerk to the Burgh of Crosshill and he would also later become Clerk to the Burgh of Govanhill, and he was probably responsible for the extensions and additions to the house. He helped resist Glasgow's expansionist tendencies at least five times in the 1870s. Robertson lived at the house until 1894, during that time he would have seen Crosshill expand greatly until it became *'a thriving town of villas'*, the original village had disappeared and been largely forgotten by this time.

Crosshill House was also home for a number of years to Archbishop John Maguire who was the first Bishop of Glasgow of Irish heritage, and one of the trustees of Holy Cross Church on Dixon Avenue. He lived in Crosshill House until his death in 1920. During his residency, the house was often referred to as the Episcopal Palace, a name that was still used on maps, even after Maguire passed away, so there are clearly other residents still to be identified.

The final known resident of the house was Thomas Clarkson, a director of the Scottish Standard Oil company until 1931.

The house remained vacant for a number of years, until it was demolished in 1948. The only clues remaining to indicate the presence of the original house are the gateposts which can be seen on Crosshill Avenue. The red-brick cottages that occupy the site where the house stood, built around 1949/50, were designed by Robert Bradbury, Glasgow's director of housing. The design of those cottages won a Festival of Britain award of merit in 1951.

Charles Mitchell
Photographer

One of the most unusual and delightful buildings on Victoria Road is situated near the park, on the corner of Torrisdale Street just next to the entrance to Queen's Park station.

Built around 1890, this mock-Tudor style building, which is now a betting shop, was originally known as Queen's Park Studio, a photographic studio owned by Charles Mitchell, a highly successful society photographer.

Mitchell was born in 1848, and started his career on the east coast, in Forfar, in the 1870s. Success must have come early, because his advertising indicates that he promoted himself as a photographer *'to the nobility, clergy and gentry of Forfar and neighbourhood'* and ensured that he could engage other photographers to work under his name.

Around 1889, Mitchell moved to Glasgow, almost certainly in order to take advantage of new opportunities afforded by the imminent expansion of the city. As a renowned photographer, he would have the means to pay for, and the creative flair to commission, a very unique building, not just the studio facing onto Victoria Road but also the adjoining house, on what is now Torrisdale Street (formerly Prince Albert Street) built in a similar style, which would attract the attention of the prosperous residents of Crosshill and Govanhill, and was conveniently situated next to the recently-built train station, which would have ensured his business's visibility to the many people visiting Queen's Park.

In fact, the earliest known photograph of Queen's Park Station was probably taken by Mitchell or one of his employees, around 1890, from the window of his new studio.

Some of his early advertising indicates that he offered a quality of service that would not have come cheaply. His work was:

> Enamelled in the Parisian style which, for permanence and excellence of finish cannot be surpassed. Photographs in the Rembrandt and other styles printed in silver, platinum, or bromide.

Mitchell's surviving photographs, or carte de visite or cabinet photos, as they were often referred to, reveal that he enjoyed the patronage of a prosperous clientele, eager to present themselves in the best possible light. Carte de visites or the slightly larger cabinet photos, were used almost like business cards now, and eagerly exchanged by people who were keen to display, either in albums or on cabinets, images of their influential and prosperous friends or business colleagues.

Mitchell's business continued to thrive throughout the 1890s and he opened two other studios in Glasgow, and one in Greenock.

In 1899, at the height of the Boer War, the staff at the Queen's Park studio contributed £3 and six shillings to the war effort in South Africa.

On a personal level, Mitchell's home life seemed to be similarly productive. In 1895, a notice in the births column of the *Glasgow Herald*, indicated that a Mrs Mitchell, resident of Queen's Park Studios, gave birth to twin girls.

The introduction of the Kodak Box Brownie in 1900, ushered in a new era in photography, an increase in people taking their own photographs, which would have impacted Mitchell's business. Whether he continued working beyond then is unknown, but when he died in 1904, the notice in the press indicate that he was living on Mansionhouse Road in Langside.

The business continued beyond his death, whether it was a family member that took over, or another photographer trading under the Mitchell name is unknown, but older residents of Govanhill have confirmed that the building continued to be used as a photographic studio until the late 1950s or early 1960s.

Govanhill Recreation Grounds & Govanhill Park

When Govanhill became a burgh in 1877, the land bounded by Victoria Road, Calder Street and Smith Street (now Inglefield Street) which had previously been part of the extensive Coplawhill Nursery, lay largely unused, awaiting permanent development. Coplaw Street had not yet been completed.

Throughout the 1880s and the 1890s, Glasgow Corporation was keen to absorb or 'annexe' the Burgh of Govanhill, bring it under its control. For a long time, Govanhill resisted those advances but one of the promises Glasgow made to the Burgh of Govanhill, to persuade them to join forces with their larger neighbour, was that the Coplawhill area would finally be developed, new houses would be built, and Govanhill could expand.

Govanhill insisted that the new estate would not be over-developed, but that the Corporation provided a public park within the new estate.

Glasgow agreed, but Coplawhill was a prime building location, the land for the new park did not come cheaply, the four and a half acres required cost the city £12,000 to purchase, in large part, from the Hutcheson's Hospital Trust.

Work had already started on the transformation of Coplawhill in 1893, an extensive stone-breaking yard was set up and hundreds of unemployed were put to work making bricks.

Work commenced on the new park in 1894 and the Parks Department decided that, unlike other parks in the city, there would be a focus on recreation for children in the new park.

Referred to as Govanhill Recreation Grounds originally, the new park opened in 1896 and was divided into two levels, on one level, the level nearer Smith Street, was a gravel pitch for football games, for boys under twelve, on the higher level, nearer Langside Road, was a gymnasium, or what became known as the swings. In the centre of the park was a small building, housing a park-keepers office and toilets. A path ran around the perimeter of the park and the borders were decorated with trees and shrubbery.

In 1912, a modern bandstand was added to the lower part of the park, a more modern bandstand than the one that stood in Queen's Park at the time.

At the opening ceremony, on 3rd of June, William Lorimer, chairman of the North British Locomotive Company and staunch Govanhillian, who had contributed £170 to the cost of construction, said:

...the Corporation have devoted themselves with great zeal to very many activities on behalf of the citizens, and it was just possible that there might be some difference of opinion as to the expediency and wisdom of some of those, but there could be absolutely no difference of opinion as to the expediency and wisdom of providing open-air music for the people in the various districts in Glasgow. We would like if occasionally the bands would play choruses in which the children could join in singing and music to which the children could dance. It was only fair and reasonable that the music should be presented in a form agreeable and helpful to everybody.

Apart from performances at the bandstand, Govanhill Recreation Grounds served in its main function as a public park, but rarely to the attention of the newspapers.

One notable exception occurred in 1959, when there was a procession to celebrate the centenary of the nearby Seventh Cameronian regiment, based at the Drill Hall on Coplaw Street, formerly the home of Third Lanark Volunteers, and there must have been many more public and civic events that took place but unfortunately, have been lost to history.

By the 1980s, the park was in serious decline; in common with many other public facilities around Glasgow it had begun to suffer from under-investment and a lack of care and attention, the original swings had been removed and the bandstand was covered in graffiti.

In 1996, the park was closed temporarily and redesigned. A new, reimagined and reinvigorated park, opened on the 27 of June 1997, and is today a much-used and much-loved feature of modern Govanhill.

The Govanhill and Crosshill District Library

The Govanhill and Crosshill District Library opened on 16th March 1906, the ninth of 15 district libraries established around Glasgow, thanks in part to a gift of £115,000 from philanthropist Andrew Carnegie.

The library was designed by architect James Rhind, in an Edwardian Baroque style. The main entrance to the library was on Langside Road.

Originally, there was a reading department with space for 10,000 books and which held 29 daily and 31 weekly newspapers, 36 weekly periodicals, 44 monthly magazines, and 550 reference books.

There was a general reading room, a ladies' reading room, a boys' reading room and a girls' reading room. The entrance to the children's reading room was on Calder Street.

The land cost £2,000, the building cost £7,000 and the first stock of books cost £1,200. In 1906, the estimated annual expenditure was £800.

A printed catalogue of all the books available in the library was available for one penny, which revealed an astonishing range of subjects.

In 1912, an 18-year-old local boy called Allan Rue, was arrested for stealing 129 maps, three books and 33 pages from three volumes dealing with poison.

During his trial Rue stated that he intended to travel and wished to become acquainted with the countries he wished to visit. He was sentenced to 30 days in prison. What direction his future career took has yet to be established.

The catalogue also included byelaws about the standards of behaviour expected in libraries. Bye-law number four stated:

No person who is intoxicated, uncleanly in person or clothing, or who is suffering from an infectious or offensive disease, shall enter or be allowed to remain in any library. No audible conversation shall be permitted in any Reading Room nor shall any person partake of refreshments, whistle, smoke, spit, or sleep therein, or bring in any animal, or any cycle, or other cumbrous or inconvenient article; and no person shall interfere with the arrangements for conducting the library, or with the comfort of any readers therein, or use the library for any purposes other than those for which it is intended.

Other guidance was included on how to use and treat books, advising the washing of hands before reading and a stern admonition to avoid wetting the finger to turn the page.

Another directive in the catalogue, reveals one of the public health concerns of the time:

Should infectious disease occur in houses where there are library books, the books or borrower's ticket must not be returned to the library but handed over to any officer of the Sanitary Authority for disinfection or destruction.

There is an unconfirmed story, in more recent years, that the small statue of a winged figure on top of the dome above the library, was stolen when the value or the material was revealed in a newspaper article. It was subsequently found abandoned in a side-street, presumably too difficult to sell. It is claimed that when the statue was reinstated on top of the dome, it was not put back facing the same direction that it had originally.

In 2015, The Diversity Project created a display of stained-glass windows which tells the story of local people and is on permanent display in the library.

Now the library caters for one of the most ethnically diverse communities in Glasgow.

The Holy Cross Mission

The first Catholic mission in Crosshill was the Holy Cross chapel-at-ease on Daisy Street, built in 1882. As a chapel-at-ease, it was designed to meet the needs of the growing Catholic population within the area who could not easily attend services at other more established parish churches elsewhere, such as St John's in the Gorbals. The new building had a dual purpose, to serve as a chapel and a school.

The Education Act of 1872 had introduced compulsory education under the management of parish school boards, but Catholic authorities opted out of the national system, preferring to appoint governors approved by the church, usually the parish priest.

In 1882, Hannah Power was appointed teacher-in-charge, and the opening ceremony took place on 4 June 1883. *The Scottish Catholic Directory* reported:

A new school has opened to meet the needs of the increasing Catholic population of the vicinity who had previously to attend St John's. It contains one large hall used as a classroom for weekdays and a chapel for Sundays. The benches are so arranged that they serve the double purpose of seats for the congregation and school desks. The building was carried out to the design of Messrs Pugin and Pugin, Westminster by Mr John Devlin, contractor, of Glasgow. The amount of the contract was £1750. On the opening day, Archbishop Eyre preached at High Mass.

In 1884, Ms Power was joined by two new staff, Sophia Stromner and first year pupil-teacher M. Haggerty. Two years later, the congregation had grown sufficiently for Holy Cross to become an independent mission. The first priest-in charge was Father Peter Link, a German, who had come to Scotland as a result of Bismarck's anti-religious legislation.

There was as yet no presbytery, so Father Link rented a flat in a tenement at 36 Garturk Street, which allowed him to live in the area, and he presided over the beginning of a period of rapid expansion and growth in Crosshill and Govanhill.

Father Link's tenure was short, and he was succeeded by Rev. William O'Brien in 1889. Father O'Brien was a man of vision and energy, and he was blessed with the support of a growing and enthusiastic congregation.

In 1895, Devon Villa, a large mansion on Albert Road was purchased for use as a presbytery, it was also clear that the chapel school was no longer sufficient for the growing congregation and expansion was required.

In 1898, work started on a second, larger chapel school on the site immediately adjoining the first, what is now Daisy Street Neighbourhood Centre. The ground floor was for the school and the second floor was for the chapel. The new building finally opened on 16 September 1900. The total cost was £8,500 of which the congregation had raised £3,500.

The first chapel school became a parochial hall known as The Institute.

The population was growing rapidly, and soon after opening it was realised that the new chapel school would be needed for educational purposes alone. In 1905, a three-day fundraising bazaar was held at City Halls and an enthusiastic congregation had raised £1,500 before the event.

Two sites were considered for the new church, both on Dixon Avenue, one at the corner of Daisy Street, the other on Belleisle Street. Eventually the site on Belleisle Street was preferred but local people on Dixon Avenue objected, claiming that an assembly of Irish people in the area, on their street, would lead to a devaluation of their property.

Perhaps because of these objections, the Dean of Guild refused planning permission but an appeal to the Court of Session was successful, and building went ahead. The new church cost £8,000 and the presbytery cost £2,000 and opened on 26 November 1911.

Large crowds were expected to attend the first mass that admission was by ticket only. Tickets were priced at 10s 5d. The final mass at the chapel school was held on the same day.

The original chapel school was later converted into a supplementary school.

The Marie Stuart Hall
(371 Langside Road)

The first block of flats on the southern side of Queen Mary Avenue (numbers 2 – 10), at the junction with Langside Road, look like an ordinary block of flats but this building once had a quite different purpose, it was a public hall, and the main entrance was on Langside Road.

According to the title deeds for one of the flats at this address, the land was first made available for development in 1861, but there is no evidence yet discovered that any construction work took place in that decade.

In the mid-1870s, renowned Victorian photographer, George Washington Wilson, captured an image of the view towards Glasgow, from the top of Queen's Park, and in that image, the block at the corner of Queen Mary Avenue is clearly seen, under construction. Wilson's photograph is only dated on the University of Aberdeen's website, as pre-1877, but other events in the neighbourhood, when taken into account, allow a more accurate date to be established, for the photograph, and for the construction of the hall.

In 1873, a short distance away on Victoria Road, a Masonic brotherhood called the Marie Stuart Lodge (Lodge number 541), consecrated their new premises in a hall above the Queen's Park Restaurant, approximately where the Tron Church is now situated.

In 1874, a fire started in the restaurant and destroyed the entire block and other surrounding buildings, including a billiard hall and a bagatelle saloon. The Marie Stuart Lodge were forced to hold their meetings in Mr Watson's School Room, sometimes called Watson's Academy, situated on Langside Road, which was somewhere between numbers 329 to 346. This, though, was only a temporary arrangement until more permanent premises became available. The opportunity to move did not happen immediately, despite all the construction work locally, but sometime, probably in 1875, construction work began on the site at the corner of Langside Road and Queen Mary Avenue.

The building must have been completed in late 1876 (and Wilson's photograph taken several months earlier) because an article in the *North British Daily Mail* on the 23rd of December that year, notes the consecration of the new premises belonging to the Marie Stuart Lodge and goes on to describe the interior:

> It has just been constructed by Mr Thomas Renton, of Crosshill, is 50 feet in length by 30 feet wide, with a high coned ceiling and tastefully decorated with elegant cornices and plaster decorations. It is capable of accommodating between 200 and 300 persons and its acoustic qualifications are excellent.

The rental fee from this hall when it was not being used by the Masons, would have certainly helped the Lodge pay the rates and other bills that were associated with the building.

Only a limited number of the events that took place in the hall have so far been discovered in press notices. Some examples include for instance that in March 1877, the local licenced grocers met there to discuss the new Intoxicating Liquor Act; in April 1877, the St. Ninian's Church Choir, led by a Mr Schob, delivered a performance which included piano recitals and readings from Dickens. In 1898, the Queen's Park Cycling Club held their AGM there, and in 1914, there were local election hustings for the Langside Ward.

In time, other public spaces would have been built and eventually the popularity and viability of the hall began to wane. In 1912, it was considered as a venue for an electric theatre, in other words a cinema, but a purpose-built venue on Smith Street was chosen instead.

There is no mention of Masonic activity after 1914, and for several years, the hall is listed as the address of The Hebrew Mission, a Christian organisation seeking to convert Jews. Then from 1932 to around 1946 it was the headquarters of the south-eastern division of the Glasgow Girl Guides.

After 1946, there is no further mention in local directories of the Marie Stuart Hall but the address, number 371 Langside Road, is by this time the registered address of the Strathclyde Hosiery Company. That company may have been the proprietors, however photographic evidence (the only photograph that exists of 371 Langside Road) suggests that the building hosted other tenants in the clothing trade, including one called Costume and Clothing.

From 1960, number 371 Langside Road is no longer listed, so what was the hall likely became a workshop or storage space for business operating from Queen Mary Avenue, particularly between numbers 4 and 8. Some of those business included Walter Crighton, a textile agent and drapery and textile manufacturer, the O'Hagen Brothers, who were wholesale suppliers, the Meta Bespoke and Surgical Footwear Company, the Stewarton Hosiery Company and Boyd and Matier's, a painting and decorating company.

In more recent years, there was also a joinery business there, an antique business run by Mr. James Barnes. The entrance to that business was on Queen Mary Avenue. By all accounts, Mr Barnes was very keen on collecting or playing bagpipes.

Anecdotal evidence suggests that in the early 1980s, the block lay empty and unused for a while, but in 1985 it was converted to residential use once again.

At the very top of the gable end on Langside Road, there is a slight trace of the sign for the old Marie Stuart Hall and above the first-floor windows, there are tantalising glimpses, behind the flaking paint, of the old shop signs which, though they are currently impossible to read, provide a hint at the building's long storied history.

Queen's Park Station and Crosshill Station

'God made the country, man made the cities, and the railways made the suburbs' is the opening line of R.W. Campbell's fictional tale about the Cathcart Railway, published in 1919, called *Snooker Tam and the Cathcart Railway*, in which young Tam, serving on the line during the First World War, encounters a German spy.

The short novel goes onto suggest just how important the line became, at least to Glaswegians:

> The Cathcart Railway is as famous as the Grand Trunk Road or Watling Street. To be ignorant of the Cathcart Circle is akin to saying that the Thames is in Germany and that Tweed is in Alaska. After the Polis Force the Cathcart Railway is the greatest thing in Glesca.

The opening of Queen's Park in the 1860s accelerated the growth and development of new suburbs on the south side of the River Clyde, including Govanhill and Crosshill.

That process continued on in the 1870s and the 1880s. Not long after Central Station opened in 1879, proposals were made to build a suburban railway line, which would link the city centre to those suburbs and provide an alternative to horse-drawn trams, and even bring outlying districts within reach of the metropolis, districts which would, it was hoped, within a few years, become part of Glasgow.

Three rival companies bid for the right to build the line, which would be Scotland's first suburban railway line. The bidding process, gaining parliamentary and local approval, would take over three years.

When residents of Govanhill and Crosshill were consulted, some were hesitant, concerned about the value of their property but when it was suggested that if the opportunities afforded by the railway were declined, the progress that had been enjoyed in the district in recent years would be lost, setback at least ten years, then approval was near unanimous.

The bid was won by the Cathcart District Railway Company, whose Chairman George Browne, also the Provost of Crosshill, was keen that his burgh would benefit from the close connection to the city, afforded by the railway.

The building process would take another three years but eventually the Cathcart line opened on the 1st of March

1886. Although the plan was for the line to eventually circle back to Central Station, at first it only went as far as Cathcart, on its way there, passing through Govanhill and Crosshill.

The original plan was for six stations on the line to Cathcart, but only five were built. There was going to be a station on Pollokshaws Road, and another on Victoria Road, but the project from the beginning was beset with challenges and difficulties, so, in order to save money and speed up construction, only five were built, the Pollokshaws Road Station was abandoned but the Victoria Road entrance to the Queen's Park Station led to a long platform, the longest platform on the line, at the end of which was another entrance, only a short distance from Pollokshaws Road.

Also, what we know now as Queen's Park Station, was originally going to be called Crosshill Station and Crosshill Station was originally going to be called Govanhill (Cathcart Road) Station, but the names we know now were finalised before the line opened.

Queen's Park Station cut through a large nursery called Hutchenson's Gardens, owned by the Hutchenson's Hospital Trust, which was one of the most significant landowners in the area. An early photograph of the station, taken around 1889 or 1890, shows the station, with some of the gardens still on the north side of the line, before they sold up entirely and allowed tenements to be built on the land.

The retaining walls at most stations proved very difficult and time-consuming to construct, and it was a major challenge to ensure they could do the job required, but there is no retaining wall on the north side of the line at Queen's Park Station, just a grass slope, possibly as a result of a mason's strike, or simply just the continued presence of the nursery. This resulted in a more open feel at that station, but that was not possible at the next stop, Crosshill, where the station had to fit between existing buildings, and as a result is the narrowest platform on the line.

The platform at Queen's Park was wide enough to accommodate a ticket office, a signal box, even a bookseller's stall, owned at first by someone called F.W. Wilson. At Crosshill, the ticket office had to be built at street level, with just a small, narrow waiting room and signal box on the platform. The ticket office there was demolished in the early 1960s and a smaller ticket office was placed within the platform's waiting room.

One of the most significant challenges, one that could not be avoided, came on the section of the line between Queen's Park and Crosshill, the challenge of building under the existing tenements on Victoria Road. Elsewhere on the line, some buildings had been taken down to make way for the line, but there was no question of demolishing the tenements on Victoria Road, which had only been constructed a decade or so earlier. A tunnel was excavated under the tenements, which were supported by underpinning, with steel beams which effectively created a bridge.

The Cathcart line was extended in 1894, circling back to Central Station and the Cathcart District Railway company maintained their independence until 1921, when the new Railways Act forced smaller companies to amalgamate with larger companies, and the Cathcart line came under control of the London, Midland and Scottish Railway company. Then in 1948, nationalisation brought all the railways in Britain under government control.

Electrification was first considered by the Cathcart District Railway Company as early as 1889 and again, on a number of occasions in the following years, but the idea was shelved each time, due to the costs and potential disruption to the service. After nationalisation, large-scale electrification was finally approved across the city. Lines on the north side of the river were converted first but on the 10th of December 1961, after two years of work, and much disruption, electric power was switched on around the Cathcart Circle.

The retaining wall at Queen's Park had to be extended, in order to accommodate the necessary equipment, and at Crosshill, the entire platform, including the waiting room had to be lowered to allow sufficient clearance under the bridge at Cathcart Road.

After that, the new blue electric trains became a regular sight on the line, but steam trains were kept in reserve until the electric trains proved reliable. On more than one occasion, the new trains broke down and were towed, ignominiously, by the steam trains they were designed to replace, through Queen's Park and Crosshill.

Around 1990, the platform at Queen's Park was truncated, shortened by around forty metres, and replaced with a wire fence leading to the steps on the west side of the station, at Niddrie Road. Establishing the reason why the platform was shortened has been difficult; some former railway employees suggest it was part of a general cost-cutting programme, others have suggested that changing train lengths may have been a factor.

The Cathcart Circle has survived periods of uncertainty, of privatisation and austerity but remains a popular and even vital travel option for thousands of people living on the south side of Glasgow every year. In the year 2019 to 2020, there were nearly 800,000 journeys starting or ending at Queen's Park and around 363,000 from Crosshill. Those figures inevitably declined during the pandemic but will surely return to pre-pandemic levels soon.

Queen's Park

In the early 1850s, the population of Glasgow was growing rapidly, the city was expanding westwards, so a decision was made to build a public park, near Kelvingrove. The city was also expanding southwards, in particular, into the Gorbals and Laurieston districts. The south side was at this time, home to about 100,000 people, a quarter of the population of Glasgow. Even before work on Kelvingrove started, there were calls for a similar park on the south side of the river.

The Town Council promised that as soon as the accounts regarding Kelvingrove were settled then they would begin work on a park for the south side. The suburbs were expanding rapidly, and so the pressure was on to find a suitable, available plot of land.

New industries, property developers, speculators and railway companies, were snapping up land as soon as it became available, and so for the council there was little option but to consider land outside the city limits.

Land to the south of Langside was considered, but was ultimately rejected because it was too prone to flooding from the River Cart.

A less flood-prone and largely undeveloped plot of land was identified, south of Eglinton Toll, between Cathcart Road to the east and Pollokshaws Road to the west, and stretching south to Camp Hill, the only real obstacle being the Coplawhill Nursery. If some had had their way the entire land in question from Eglinton Toll to Camphill would have become a public park, but the cost of developing and constructing the park could only be recouped by feuing the surrounding land for housing, as had been the case in Kelvingrove, so in the end a much smaller portion of that land, the Lands of Pathhead Farm, some 143 acres, owned by Neil Thompson, were purchased by the council for £30,000.

The extravagance of purchasing land beyond Glasgow's boundaries was criticised by some, both within the council and in the press, but the argument was won by those who observed that the suburbs were expanding rapidly, and they wisely considered that it would only be a matter of time before any new park lay within the city boundaries.

In 1857, a journalist writing in the *Glasgow Sentinel* said of the proposed lands on which the new park would be built:

the only drawback is that they are a few minutes beyond the adjoining suburbs but as the said suburb is hurrying out of town as fast as it can, this is an evil which will very soon cure itself.

An additional problem was that there was no existing direct route to the site of the city's new 'lung', meaning no easy way for the citizens of Glasgow to reach their new park. To remedy this, a new road and bridge would have to be constructed, a continuation of Eglinton Street, which would cross the Glasgow, Neilston and Barrhead railway line, which had been constructed in the previous decade, to serve the Southside Railway Station, near Gushetfaulds.

The celebrated designer, Sir Joseph Paxton who had designed Crystal Palace in London and Kelvingrove Park in Glasgow, put forward an ambitious design for the new park and the surrounding area which would sweep away all previous ideas.

Paxton wrote:

Having had many parks to lay out, and having visited nearly all the public parks in Europe, it has always occurred to me that there was a want of what I consider ought to be an essential feature in such places of resort, that is, a covered building to shelter visitors from the weather, and which should also be an attractive object in itself. In our climate especially it often happens that those who go out for recreation and exercise are over-taken by rain, and having no place of shelter, suffer serious inconvenience, and, frequently, instead of deriving the benefit to their health of which they went in search, are laid up, for several days, from the effects of cold and wet, and sometimes sustain permanent injury to their health. I have, accordingly, provided in my design for the erection of a handsome, but not expensive building, which will entirely obviate this difficulty.

I propose the central part of the building to be used for a variety of purposes. Its general use I would recommend to be as a museum for works of art, and it could also be appropriated to periodical exhibitions, musical promenades, and various other purposes during the summer. I propose to cover the two wings with glass, and to plant a good-sized border at the back of each with plants from Australia, China, the Himalayas, and other temperate climes, so as to form a beautiful screen to the back wall, and at the same time leave room for a promenade of sufficient width to make a most agreeable resort at all seasons. The plants would be such as to require very little expense or care to keep in order. The end buildings would be appropriated for refreshment-rooms and cloak-rooms, and provided with other necessary conveniences, and a rental would be derived from letting them to a contractor.

Paxton's *'handsome but not expensive'* building was actually a very grand Winter Garden. His design also included a new route to the park, which was in a direct line from Eglinton Street, Langside Road would be diverted around the hill, previously it went straight over the hill, all the way to the village of Langside. There would be space for villas, even as far east as what is now known as Cathkin Park, and a large artificial lake on the south side of the park, near the village of Langside.

In the early stages of planning the future park was simply referred to as the South Side Park but at a town council meeting in June 1857, a motion was put forward by the real champion of the effort in local government, Baillie Gemmill, a councillor in the Gorbals and Convenor of the Parks Committee. Gemmill proposed to call the new park, Queen's Park, not in honour of Queen Victoria, but of Mary Queen of Scots, because she had fought her final battle, the Battle of Langside, on the southern slopes of the park, near the village of Langside. There was little opposition to celebrating those historical associations, but there was some debate about the name of the new approach road; some including the Lord Provost, thought Queen's Drive would be *'a more graceful appellation'* and put forward an amendment to the motion. In the end, both parts of Baillie Gemmill's motion passed by the closest of margins, 22 to 19, and the Queen's Park and Victoria Road were christened.

Work started in earnest shortly afterwards, when the Parks Department approved £28,350 for the preparation and laying out of the park. The Superintendent of Parks, Duncan McLellan, recruited a small army of unemployed or under-employed labourers. The first task involved a long period of simply clearing and draining the land, making it ready for building and landscaping. A further £4,750 was also approved for the building of the new road and bridge – a Mr. Struthers was commissioned to build the road and a Mr. Nielsen to build the bridge.

Paxton's proposal for the approach road was a grand boulevard that was 150 feet wide, lined with trees and stretching from the Broomielaw, all the way to the gates of the new park. This new thoroughfare would cut through land owned principally by William Dixon and by Hutcheson's Hospital Trust, who were naturally keen to extract as much value from their property by allowing developers to build houses, churches and tenements, but a wide boulevard would naturally restrict opportunities for building.

Dixon, by many accounts, an argumentative, combative man, became so infuriated with the negotiation process that he was barred from attending, and had to delegate the task to his lawyers. In the end, after lengthy negotiations, the idea of a tree-lined boulevard was quietly dropped and the width of Victoria Road was reduced to a more modest 100 feet.

Paxton did get his tree-lined boulevard within the boundaries of the park and some other features he proposed were adopted, such as the route of the roads and the pathways within the park, but his more grandiose ideas, specifically the lake and winter garden, were postponed. Those ideas were never formally rejected, just put into abeyance until some future date, when enough money would be available. Even in the 1890s, when the park was expanded, there was still hope that Paxton's plan could still be realised.

To make the park a reality, City Architect John Carrick and Park Supervisor Duncan McLellan, had to work within their means, and also incorporate other ideas, other features considered essential or desirable in the new design. Surplus soil, removed during the landscaping of the lower parts of the new park was taken to the peak of the hill to form a mound upon which a flagpole was raised, around which a spectacular, previously unavailable view of the surrounding countryside, for several miles in all directions, could be enjoyed.

One contemporary commentator, standing at the new flagpole described the newly formed vista:

From this point, the view is one of we may call it, almost unparalleled beauty, and the spectator seems to be standing on a tower looking around on all sides upon ample expanses of country. In the foreground lies Glasgow, with its great counterpane of smoke resting above it like a cloud. Its gigantic stalks, its steeples, its forest of masts and its dense pile of human dwellings. To the north and west of the city the eye reaches the distant Kilpatrick hills and the rounder and 'burlier' outlines of the Campsie range, which close the view in these directions. Sweeping to the east along the Vale of Clyde, it traverses a panorama of magnificent scenery with the double head of Tinto marked out against the horizon and Lanark dimly visible at its feet. A shoulder of the finely wooded Cathkin Braes, lying only two or three miles from the park, intercepts the view of the distant country just where the eye meets Lanark, but the rich variety outline and undulation which these hills present, their exuberance of fertile beauty, form one of the most striking features in the vast landscape which the mound commands.

The southern slope of the park, and of Camphill on one side and the western slope of the Cathkin Braes on the other, meet in a hollow basin through which flows the Cart, and which gradually widens into a short valley, opening up a prospect into the district of Mearns, Eaglesham and the famous Drumclog. On the west rises the hill of Ballageich, a name bearing a strong resemblance to one familiar to all readers of Scottish history. Around the western base of the hill, over which the park extends, cluster the populous manufacturing towns of Paisley, Pollokshaws, Barrhead Neilston etc., which by the erection of the mound have been brought into view, but which by the Camphill, were previously not visible from the park.

The park opened informally in the summer of 1862, and as many 25,000 people a day visited regularly, even though the park was still very much a work in progress. The formal opening took place on the 11th of September of that year, and Queen's Park took its place as the third public park in Glasgow.

The Parks Committee, including ex-Bailie Gemmill, Convenor of the Parks Committee, Bailie Whyte, Colonel Dreghorn, Dr Joshua Paterson, Dr Strang and City Architect, John Carrick, drove by carriage from the city, along Eglinton Street and Victoria Road and into the park. There was no iron fence at that point, just a simple hedge marking the boundaries of the park. Inside the park, they immediately turned westward and followed the carriage drive over the high ground to Langside and back to the main gate. From there they walked up the boulevard and then onto the flagstaff where speeches were made to the assembled crowd. Bailie Gemmill stated, on the authority of Joseph Paxton, that:

when the park is finally completed, it will be unsurpassed, if even equalled by any public recreation ground in Europe.

At some point during the proceedings, the councillors also found time to plant a chestnut tree, in the north-west corner of the park. That chestnut tree still stands proudly at the entrance to the Wellcroft Bowling Club.

A total of 143 acres had been purchased to create Queen's Park but at this point did not include the Camphill Estate. Around 25 acres of land was reserved for the Recreation Grounds and over 30 acres was reserved for housing, leaving around 90 acres for the main section of the park.

The land reserved for housing was divided into multiple plots and would, the Council hoped, be sold or feued to developers, providing money which would recoup the cost of building and laying out the park in the first place, as had been the case at Kelvingrove Park, a few years earlier.

The land immediately around the park, principally what is now Queen's Drive would not be made available for feuing until 1865, when the first phase of the park development was complete, but that did not stop speculators, almost as soon as construction started in 1859, building as close to the new green space as they could, on Victoria Road and the new streets that would soon be laid out.

This progress did not please everyone particularly the residents of Crosshill who were keen to preserve their idyllic, rural retreat. One wrote to a newspaper in 1861:

the eye is offended at every turn. Everywhere there is evidence of bad taste and disregard to the interests of the locality.

The disgruntled residents of Crosshill could not stop their little village becoming a much busier place, even though some tried.

In fact, because so many people wanted to live close to the new park, developers, builders and architects prospered and within a few short years, Crosshill became what was often described as a 'town of villas'. With this prosperity, came prestige and self-confidence and Crosshill would soon become an independent and self-governing burgh.

Work began on building houses on Queen's Drive in 1865, but that work was not finally complete until 1886, when Balmoral Terrace opened, very close to the original gates to the park on Victoria Road. In those early days, the park and the joining Recreation Grounds would have been used and enjoyed, not just by local residents but by many from further afield, who would travel to enjoy one of the few open spaces freely available to citizens of Glasgow.

The main park would have been popular with all classes of society; for some it would have been a place to take a carriage ride or to be seen by or meet other respectable members of society. For the middle and working classes it would have been a place to enjoy a little fresh air, some respite from the daily grind and the polluted air of the city, and a wide open space that would inevitably tempt all kinds of human behaviour.

Within a year of opening the council had to issue a series of byelaws, specifically related to Queen's Park, to prohibit certain types of undesirable activity:

1. No person shall enter or leave the park except by the ordinary gates.

2. No persons shall use any part of the park with horses and mules or asses, carriages or vehicles of any description, except on the roads laid out as carriage drives.

3. No person shall take any dog into the park unless it be led by the party in charge.

4. All furious riding or driving is prohibited.

5. No groom or horse breaker shall exercise or train any horse in any part of the park.

6. No person shall cut or injure or pull up or deface any of the trees, shrubs, flowers, grass, turf fences, fountains or seats in any part of the park.

7. Certain portions of the park consisting of artificial sloping terraces, fringed with flowers and shrubs, being very liable to injury, persons are strictly prohibited from walking, running, lying or being upon any part of the set slopes or flower grounds bearing the intimation " Please keep off the grass".

8. No games of any kind shall be played in or upon any part of the park, except upon such portions there off as are specially set apart for that purpose.

9. No person shall enter or use any part of the Park Road leading from Pollokshaws Road to where it joins Cathcart Road with lorries, carts, spring vans, or barrows.

10. The park shall be open from 1st April to 30th September inclusive, from six o'clock morning till ten o'clock evening and from 1st October to 31st March inclusive from 7 o'clock morning till 7 o'clock evening.

11. Any person contravening any part of the sixth by-law shall, insofar as otherwise provided be liable, to a penalty not exceeding £5 for each offence, and any person contravening any part of the other bylaws above specified shall be liable to a penalty not exceeding 20 shillings for each offence.

Further prohibitions were imposed a year or so later, when a new craze called cycling emerged. There had been experimental cycling machines for a few years previously, but mass production of velocipedes encouraged a new enthusiasm among people for the activity and soon it was forbidden to ride your velocipede, penny farthing, bicycle or tricycle within Queen's Park – this rule was not relaxed until the 1880s.

The Recreation Grounds

Very few early events held on the Recreation Grounds have been recorded but one of the first ever organised dog shows in Scotland took place there in 1864; there was also horse racing, hammer throwing, rounders, cricket and even golf.

Glasgow Golf Club was formed in 1787 and played originally on Glasgow Green, but the need for recreational space in the growing city of Glasgow was intense, which meant the sport could not continue at Glasgow Green, and the club folded in the 1830s.

By 1870, some members of the Prestwick Golf Club, formed in 1851, lived and worked in Glasgow, and were keen to establish a club closer to the city, and so the Glasgow Golf Club was reconstituted and the Recreation grounds were chosen as the site of a new course.

Charlie Hunter, the professional from Prestwick, laid out a 9-hole course but there were no bunkers at this stage. Membership was a guinea per year and a fee of £2 per year was paid to the keeper of Queen's Park Bowling Club, to look after the golf clubs and the greens.

The first match was played on the 5th of March 1870, 'Young' Tom Morris, the leading Scottish professional at the time and winner of four successive Open Championships by the age of 21, joined the Lord Provost, the captain of the club and others.

The course would not have compared favourably to courses of today. Lawn mowers had recently been invented but those would have been used only on the greens. The grass on the fairways would still be very long and would need to be scythed, but somehow the golfers managed and in 1873 invited another club, Leith Thistle to play a competition.

Discussions moved on to building a clubhouse and the Parks Department granted permission for a building to be constructed, but the sport was not as popular in the city as it was on the coast. The club, which, was still relatively small and afraid of accruing debt, instead decided to quit Queen's Park and move to Alexandra Park, a new park in the east end of the city, which was judged more affordable.

Enthusiasm for organised football began to gather momentum in the 1860s; on the 9th of July 1867, at a meeting at 3 Eglinton Terrace (now better known as 404 Victoria Road), the following resolution was recorded:

Tonight at half past eight o'clock a number of gentlemen met at No. 3 Eglinton Terrace for the purpose of forming a football club.

That football club would become known as Queen's Park Football Club, now the oldest football club in Scotland and in many ways, pioneers of the modern game of football. Queen's Park took their name from the nearby park and played their first matches on the Recreation Grounds. Their emphasis on the passing game rather than running and brute strength, earned them the nickname 'The Scotch Professors'.

The popularity of football soared after the first Scotland versus England international match, held in the west end of Glasgow in 1872. Most of the team representing Scotland were Queen's Park players. Soon after that historic, galvanising event, a multitude of clubs were formed in neighbourhoods across the city, and many on the south side chose to play at the Recreation Grounds, in fact, for many fledgling teams, it was the only free option available.

Just a few years later, in 1873, the Queen's Park team, by now established as one of the leading teams in the country, built their own stadium, a short distance away, on land feued from the Town Council, land originally part of the Queen's Park estate. This purpose-built stadium, arguably the first of its kind in the world, would become known as Hampden Park, the first of three stadiums to bear that name, because it was situated on a street called Hampden Terrace. It would play host to Queen's Park's home games and several significant international matches, including a 5 – 1 victory for Scotland over England in 1882, which is celebrated on a mural on the wall of the bowling club that now occupies the site.

The Kibble Palace

In 1871, it looked as if Queen's Park would finally get something like the Winter Gardens that Paxton proposed.

John Kibble, an inventor and photographer, from Coulport in Argyle, constructed a large conservatory on his property on the shores of Loch Long, and offered to move it at his own cost, to Glasgow and rebuild it in Queen's Park. After being allowed to run the venue as a commercial venture for 21 years, Kibble would then gift it to the city.

Kibble's generosity was welcomed and celebrated in some quarters, but almost certainly because of the influence of the Temperance movement, on the south side of Glasgow in particular, the Council hesitated, and Kibble withdrew the offer, instead coming to a private agreement with the Royal Botanical Institution, setting up the palace in the Burgh of Hillhead, which lay to the west of Glasgow.

When the Kibble Crystal Art Palace and Conservatory finally opened in 1873, Kibble revealed to the audience some of the difficulties he had faced when he made his original offer to the council. A journalist who attended that opening ceremony and heard Kibble's speech, summarised those difficulties:

> By many it was considered to be simply a winter garden of large dimensions, while others thought it was to be a place of the of resort for those who wish to lounge and smoke their cigars, and to put an enemy in their mouths to steal away their brains – persons whose unruly conduct would desecrate the neighbourhood and render it anything but an agreeable locality in which to reside. He did not think however that the nature of the erection warranted anyone in arriving at such a conclusion.

The Extension of Queen's Park in 1894

Originally, the Recreation Grounds were much larger than they are now, but over time, portions of that land (and other parts of the park) were feued or sold off for development as the Council sought to recoup the costs of purchasing, laying out and designing the park.

For instance, in 1867, the Council granted a ten-year lease to Queen's Park Bowling Club, to build a clubhouse and bowling rinks on a section on the northern edge of the grounds. The lease was renewed, and the club is still there to this day. In fact, Queen's Park Bowling Club became one of the most important venues for that sport in the country, and for nearly a century, played host to the Scottish Bowling Championships. Around the same time, they also granted space in the park to a well-established bowling club called the Wellcroft Bowling Club, who were forced to relocate because of the development of the Laurieston district.

However, bowling was only one of the many sports that had discovered a new-found popularity during this period, for a while, there were more sports clubs, based near and practicing on the Recreation Grounds, than in any other municipal park or any other part of the city but the clubhouse. The rinks and other building projects gradually reduced the space available for general sport and recreation.

The population of the area was also increasing, year on year, and as a result, by the 1880s, the Recreation Grounds were crowded throughout the week, with numerous sports and athletic clubs (and other public events) vying for space and time. On a Saturday afternoon in particular, there were often several football matches taking place at the same time and attracting numerous spectators.

More space was urgently required, if people were to continue to enjoy the freedom and the benefits to health that came from participation in sport. In 1891, Glasgow's municipal boundaries were extended southwards, and as predicted three decades earlier, Queen's Park now lay within the city; as did the neighbouring, privately owned, Camphill estate, which the council had declined to buy in 1857. There had been calls to purchase Camphill since Queen's Park opened but following the boundary extension, that case was renewed.

The sports clubs struggling for space on the Recreation Grounds were also keen for the Council to make that purchase. In 1893, over 250 sports clubs presented a petition to the council, urging them to purchase Camphill, which read:

The humble petition of the undersigned officials and representatives of athletic clubs in various districts of the city.

That the serious encroachments which have been made up on the space available for games in the Recreation Ground of the Queen's Park have had the effects of overcrowding the ground and compelling many to resort to feuing grounds in the neighbourhood. Those vacant places have been closed and although there is an ever-increasing taste among young men for outdoor exercise, and therefore a growing demand for more space.

The Recreation Ground has been more and more contracted, mostly by portions, which have been taken away for a tennis court, for the deaf school, for a church, for the Victoria Street Primary and worst of all, for a long tenement of buildings thrust into the heart of the playground.

The great number of working young men and lads who form themselves into athletic clubs for the more robust exercise obtained from cricket, rounders, football and so on, and who cannot afford to lease ground for this special use come to Queen's Park grounds, and that not only from the dense working population of the Southside but from all parts of the Southside as well.

Besides these regularly performed clubs there are great numbers of young men who are not associated but use the ground for the same and other athletic games with the result that many who desire opportunities for simple exercise are prevented from engaging in them by the number and by the danger of colliding with each other.

Your petitioners would for these and all the reasons urge the addition to the Queen's Park of the

ground on the summit and slopes of Camphill, and thus allow a portion of the enlarged park to be set aside for the enjoyment of quieter games and where also a gymnasium such as that one at Glasgow Green, a maze puzzle and other interesting features might be added and found advisable.

May it please your honours therefore to purchase the whole of the Camphill grounds, so as to make such addition to the Queen's Park as will relieve the overcrowded Recreation Ground and your petitioners will ever pray.

Over 250 clubs from all over Glasgow, representing thousands of people, signed the petition. The public wanted a bigger park, demanded a bigger park, and the council finally made the purchase. The acquisition of the Camphill estate for about £63,000 from Hutchenson's Hospital Trust increased the size of Queen's Park from around 90 to 148 acres.

The opening of the extended park took place on the 24th of May 1894, the newly extended Queen's Park opened to the public for the first time. A Glasgow paper wrote:

When the Police Band had ceased playing in the park crowds began moving towards the new grounds, until thousands were roaming over them, enjoying the unwonted freedom of tripping grassy meadows and squeezing through hedges without fear of tremendous penalties. On the top of a knoll on the highest slope a gigantic bonfire was lit, and the youngsters – and some old folks too – enjoyed themselves.

The additional space was very welcome but the new park soon boasted other new features; Camphill House at the centre of the estate became a museum, displaying costumes and relics from the Battle of Langside, and in the decade that followed new propagating houses and a conservatory were built, new bowling greens, two new boating ponds and in 1901, the former National Bank of Scotland was moved brick by brick from Queen Street in the centre of Glasgow, to the south-west corner of the estate, where it re-opened as Langside Halls.

Bandstands

Paxton's grand design for Queen's Park did not include a bandstand, which would have paled in comparison against his Winter Palace. Surviving council records provide no evidence of what alternatives, if any, were constructed when the park first opened, in fact, apart from Paxton's plans, there are no maps at all of Queen's Park in the 1860s or 1870s. In 1869, a letter in the *Glasgow Evening Citizen* lamented the lack of musical performances in the city's public parks, something which the writer believed, if provided, would encourage people away from '*less elevated pursuits*'.

One reply to that letter urged the council to allow bands to play in the parks and to permit boxes to be placed everywhere to collect donations. Another reply, from the leader of the Glasgow Blind Asylum Instrumental Band, claimed that his band had attempted to play in the Queen's Park the previous summer, but had been '*knocked about*' by police because they did not have an official permit.

Given the council's rejection of the Kibble Palace for Queen's Park in 1871, it seemed unlikely bandstands or music would be permitted in the parks anytime soon, but the popularity of the Kibble Palace in the Botanic Gardens, in the Burgh of Hillhead, proved that the public wanted outdoor entertainment, so, within the council, opinions began to change, and opposition quickly evaporated.

In 1872, the Music in the Parks programme is mentioned in the press for the first time. It's unlikely that the bandstands were built at this early stage, it's more likely that a simple temporary platform was provided in the summer, upon which bands could perform.

The first map to indicate there was a bandstand in Queen's Park (and all the other parks in Glasgow) is the Post Office Directory map of 1885. This original Queen's Park bandstand, of which no photo has yet been discovered, was situated well inside the park near the flagpole, close to what is now a children's southern play area. Most advertised performances were by military bands, often belonging to one or another of the many volunteer regiments stationed around Glasgow at the time, or by workplace bands.

Placing the bandstand deep inside the park did not please everyone, letters in the press indicate that having to climb the hill to reach the bandstand was considered too much for older people, even one (apparently) younger person wrote to the papers to complain too much exertion was required. One amusing reply to that letter said that if this '*lackadaisical correspondent*' sent his address to the Corporation: '*they might cart it (the bandstand) along to his backyard, so that he could enjoy the music without getting out of bed*'.

In 1891, when Govanhill and Crosshill were finally annexed to Glasgow, a note in the council minutes indicates that the City Cashier proposed moving the bandstand closer to the gates on Victoria Road, perhaps in response to public opinion, more likely, to take advantage of the extra footfall in Queen's Park that was expected upon annexation.

However, the original bandstand remained in place at the top of the hill until at least 1908. The Post Office Directory map of 1909 seems to indicate that it was removed and a new one built nearer to Victoria Road, but an Ordnance Survey map from 1913 clearly shows two bandstands in the park, a small one in the original location and a considerably larger one, near the gates at Victoria Road. It is not inconceivable that there were two bandstands in operation for a while, or that it simply took about four years for the original one to be removed.

The second bandstand, erected in late 1908 or early 1909, was constructed by the Walter McFarlane Company, who were based at the Saracen Foundry in Possilpark. This was a company that designed and forged much of Glasgow's street furniture in the Victorian and Edwardian period.

The location for the new bandstand was also criticised by some people. One irate citizen using the penname Orpheus claimed that there was a nasty echo in the vicinity and the proximity of:

> large, grey houses, noisy electric cars, parading adults and uncontrollable children does (did) not lead to successful musical concerts.

Most people were happy with the bandstand being closer to Victoria Road, but it was only there for about 14 years, until 1923. In this period, the Music in the Parks programme was expanded across Glasgow, all the traditional iron bandstands were replaced with newer, brick bandstands surrounded by specially built amphitheatres, that allowed thousands a comfortable view of the performance, there were also electrical points for amplification and around this time, some performances, from some bandstands, were broadcast on radio.

Govanhill's iron bandstand, the second bandstand in the park, was dismantled and sold to Motherwell Town Council, and it was re-erected in the Duchess of Hamilton Park, where it stood until 1949, and was then demolished, sold off for scrap.

Govanhill's third bandstand continued to host the Music in the Parks programme and other events. From around 1943, until around 1977, the bandstand was also the preferred destination for the annual May Day Rally, organised by the Scottish Trades Union Council. Notably, in 1951, Nye Bevan, founder of the NHS, spoke there about the upcoming general election.

In 1960, in one of the most celebrated concerts ever to take place in Queen's Park, Paul Robeson, the American singer, actor and political activist, who had been denied his passport during the McCarthy era because of his political beliefs, entertained an audience in the park of over ten thousand.

In 1996, the bandstand was destroyed by fire. The site remained derelict and unused until 2009, when the four local community councils surrounding the park came together and collaborated on a renovation project. In 2013, a new arena, surrounding the original amphitheatre was opened, and has revitalised the park, becoming a space for events again like the Govanhill International Festival and the Rock Against Racism 40th anniversary concert in 2016.

Events and music aside, Queen's Park is and always has been, a much-loved and even essential space for the thousands of people who live in its proximity. The park has been redeveloped numerous times, services and features have come and gone but the park remains a place to relax, to exercise, to walk and play and from the top of the hill, near the flagpole, a place to simply enjoy one of the best views of Glasgow.

During the COVID pandemic in particular, it became almost essential for the well-being of so many people, who found sanctuary, a sense of normality and peace while walking in the park. Even back in the days of heavy industry, the park was intended to be one of the city's 'lungs', a place to find a little respite and breathe fresher air and it still serves that function today.

Queen's Park is one of Glasgow's great assets so much housing has been built around this park and because of this park. Govanhill, Crosshill, and a large part of the south side would not exist in the way they do now if Queen's Park had not been built back in 1862.

Selected Bibliography

Villages of Glasgow by Aileen Smart (2002)

Minutes from the Burgh of Govanhill, 1877 – 1891 (Anon)

Captains of Industry by W.S. Murphy (1901)

Tramway and Railway World (1931)

Glasgow 1909

Scottish Referee, 1902 – 1904

Scottish Athletic Journal, 1881 – 1884

British Architect, 1881 and 1884

Historical Notices of the United Presbyterian Congregations in Glasgow edited by J.L. Aikman (1875)

100 years of Glasgow's Amazing Cinemas by Bruce Peter (1996)

Glasgow We Used to Know by David Drew (2011)

www.scottishcinemas.org.uk

References

1 The Boundary Commission Inquiry of 1885

2 Villages of Scotland: The South Side by Aileen Smart (2002)

3 Evening News, Glasgow, 17 January 1936

4 Daily Record, 29 February 1917

5 Daily Record, 29 February 1917

6 Baths and Washhouse Archive, Mitchell Library, Glasgow

Image Acknowledgements

Cover photo courtesy of Tom Pearson

Inner front cover: A map of Glasgow and the surrounding burghs in 1885, prepared for the Boundary Commissions Inquiry. Photo courtesy of Glasgow City Archives

1 Photo courtesy of Glasgow City Archives

2 ©CSG CIC Glasgow Museums and Libraries Collection: The Mitchell Library, Special Collections

3 Photo courtesy of Glasgow City Archives

4 ©CSG CIC Glasgow Museums and Libraries Collection: The Mitchell Library, Special Collections

5 Photo courtesy of Scran – part of Historic Environment Scotland

6 Source unknown

7 Photo courtesy of Scran – part of Historic Environment Scotland

8 Photo courtesy of Scran – part of Historic Environment Scotland

9 Photo courtesy of Scran – part of Historic Environment Scotland

10 Wikipedia (Creative Commons)

11 Photo courtesy of Scran – part of Historic Environment Scotland

12 Photo courtesy of Glasgow City Archives

13 Photo courtesy of Glasgow City Archives

14 Photo courtesy of Glasgow City Archives

15 Photo courtesy of Eric Eunson. Old Govanhill by Eric Eunson

16 Photo courtesy of Glasgow City Archives

17 ©CSG CIC Glasgow Museums and Libraries Collection: The Mitchell Library, Special Collections

18 ©CSG CIC Glasgow Museums and Libraries Collection: The Mitchell Library, Special Collections

19 Copyright NHS Greater Glasgow and Clyde Archives

20 Copyright NHS Greater Glasgow and Clyde Archives

21 Photo courtesy of Tom Pearson

22 Photo courtesy of Tom Pearson

23 Photo courtesy of Tom Pearson

24 Photo courtesy of Tom Pearson

25 Source unknown, public domain

26 Photo courtesy of Glasgow City Archives

27 Photo courtesy of Eric Eunson. Old Govanhill by Eric Eunson

28 Photo courtesy of Gary Painter

29 Photo courtesy of Glasgow City Archives
30 ©CSG CIC Glasgow Museums and Libraries Collection: The Mitchell Library, Special Collections
31 Photo courtesy of Gary Painter
32 Photo courtesy of Chris Doak
33 Photo courtesy of Gary Painter
34 Photo courtesy of Glasgow City Archives
35 Photo courtesy of Gary Painter
36 Photo courtesy of Eric Eunson. Old Govanhill by Eric Eunson
37 Photo courtesy of Glasgow City Archives
38 Photo courtesy of Gary Painter
39 Illustrated Sporting and Dramatic News (British Newspaper Archive)
40 Third Lanark: Champions of Scotland 1903 – 04 by Thomas Taw
41 Photo courtesy of Canmore, part of Historic Environment Scotland
42 Third Lanark: Champions of Scotland 1903 – 04 by Thomas Taw
43 British Architect Magazine, Glasgow School of Art
44 Scottish Field Magazine, March 1906
45 Gebäude für Heil- und sonstige Wohlfahrts-Anstalten (1899)
46 ©CSG CIC Glasgow Museums and Libraries Collection: The Mitchell Library, Special Collections
47 Source unknown
48 Source unknown
49 www.mgthomas.co.uk
50 Illustrated London News
51 Photo courtesy of Scran – part of Historic Environment Scotland
52 Photo by Bruce Downie
53 Photo courtesy of Glasgow City Archives
54 Photo courtesy of Glasgow City Archives
55 ©CSG CIC Glasgow Museums and Libraries Collection: The Mitchell Library, Special Collections
56 Photo courtesy of SCRAN – part of Historic Environment Scotland
57 © From the collections of the Scottish Jewish Archives Centre
58 © From the collections of the Scottish Jewish Archives Centre
59 ©CSG CIC Glasgow Museums and Libraries Collection: The Mitchell Library, Special Collections
60 Photo courtesy of Mary Gowers
61 Photo courtesy of Glasgow City Archives
62 © From the collections of the Scottish Jewish Archives Centre
63 ©CSG CIC Glasgow Museums and Libraries Collection: The Mitchell Library, Special Collections
64 Photo courtesy of Eric Eunson. Old Govanhill by Eric Eunson
65 Photo by Bruce Downie
66 National Library of Scotland
67 Wikimedia (Creative Commons). Photo by Michael Klajban
68 ©CSG CIC Glasgow Museums and Libraries Collection: The Mitchell Library, Special Collection
69 www.thelows.madasafish.com
70 www.thelows.madasafish.com
71 Photo courtesy of Eric Eunson. Old Govanhill by Eric Eunson
72 Photo courtesy of Eric Eunson. Old Govanhill by Eric Eunson
73 ©CSG CIC Glasgow Museums and Libraries Collection: The Mitchell Library, Special Collections
74 ©CSG CIC Glasgow Museums and Libraries Collection: The Mitchell Library, Special Collections
75 Photo courtesy of Canmore, part of Historic Environment Scotland
76 Photo courtesy of Eric Eunson. Old Govanhill by Eric Eunson
77 Photo courtesy of Scran – part of Historic Environment Scotland
78 The Transport Treasury
79 The Transport Treasury
80 Photo courtesy of Glasgow City Archives
81 Photo courtesy of Glasgow City Archives
82 The George Washington Wilson Collection, University of Aberdeen
83 The Graphic, 1871
84 Private Collection
85 Photo courtesy of Glasgow City Archives
86 Photo courtesy of Glasgow City Archives
87 Photo courtesy of Scran – Thomas Annan Collection. Part of Historic Environment Scotland
88 Photo courtesy of Scran – part of Historic Environment Scotland
Inner rear cover: Source unknown

88. Doorman outside the Plaza Ballroom at Eglinton Toll (1957).
Opposite: Poster for the Plaza Ballroom (c.1957).